The Policy-Making Proce
Criminal Justice System

How the state 'deals with' crime and criminality is a major issue for all students of criminology and criminal justice. This book offers a fresh perspective on the policy-making process in the criminal justice system of England and Wales by presenting a detailed overview of both the theory behind it and how it plays out in practice with contemporary policy examples.

The key features of this text include a detailed analysis of the basic political concepts surrounding the relationship between the citizen and the state as well as an overview of the state departments, organizations and individuals that are instrumental in creating and influencing policy. The book also analyses how criminal justice policy is interpreted and implemented on the street and comprises a range of discussion points and suggested further readings.

By taking a unique criminal justice-focused approach to policy making, this text is perfect for the undergraduate taking modules in criminology, criminal justice, policing, the voluntary sector and social and public policy. It will also be of interest to those who are taking more vocational routes and to practitioners.

Adrian Barton is an Associate Professor (Senior Lecturer) in Public Management and Policy at Plymouth University, UK. His background is in social policy and criminal justice. This is reflected in his primary research interests, which are substance use and child protection. He has published widely in this area, including a number of books, refereed journal articles and practice-based publications.

Nick Johns is Senior Lecturer in Social and Public Policy at Cardiff University, Wales. His research interests lie in race issues, ethnic diversity and welfare, sentencing policy and social welfare. He is co-author of *Trust and Substitutes for Trust: The Case of Britain under New Labour* (New York: Nova Science).

The Policy-Making Process in the Criminal Justice System

Adrian Barton and Nick Johns

Routledge
Taylor & Francis Group

LONDON AND NEW YORK

First published 2013
by Routledge
2 Park Square, Milton Park, Abingdon, Oxon, OX14 4RN

Simultaneously published in the USA and Canada
by Routledge
711 Third Avenue, New York, NY 10017

Routledge is an imprint of the Taylor & Francis Group, an informa business

British Library Cataloguing in Publication Data
A catalogue record for this book is available from the British Library

Library of Congress Cataloging in Publication Data
Barton, Adrian.
The policy making process in the criminal justice system / Adrian Barton and Nick Johns.
p. cm.
1. Criminal justice, Administration of--Great Britain. 2. Criminology--Great Britain. I. Johns, Nick. II. Title.
HV9960.G7B37 2012
364.941068'4--dc23
2012016746

ISBN: 978-0-415-67014-2 (hbk)
ISBN: 978-0-415-67017-3 (pbk)
ISBN: 978-0-203-10121-6 (ebk)

Typeset in Times New Roman
by Taylor & Francis Books

Printed and bound in Great Britain by the MPG Books Group

Contents

Foreword and acknowledgements

We are undeniably in a state of flux in terms of politics and policy. We have a coalition government for the first time in many decades and it is fair to say that it is working its way through a different and challenging set of working arrangements. In addition, we are seeing a global fiscal crisis manifesting in the United Kingdom as a period of austerity where government spending is being withdrawn or reduced in all areas of public provision. In addition, we are seeing a crisis in the financial stability of the eurozone and an economic slump in the USA, and the latest figures show a slowdown in China's growth. Furthermore, there is the very real prospect of the break-up of the UK with a referendum in Scotland.

Given all this, we feel that it is important that those studying aspects of public policy – of which criminology and criminal justice are undoubtedly a significant part – have a grasp of the key determinants, options, barriers and outcomes of the policy-making process in order that they better understand how and why, and, importantly, why not, certain types of policy are made and implemented. For us, an inability to do this runs the risk of creating a partial understanding of an important aspect of all governments' work.

With this in mind we set about producing this work. It was written with the express intent of giving criminal justice and criminology students a basic and accesible insight into the world of policy making. As a result we have sacrificed depth for breadth. The reasons for this are simple: this is an introductory text-book aimed at a specific group of readers. Our aims were to cover the key areas of policy making in a manner which allowed the reader to come away from the text with an understanding which, at one level, would allow them to comprehend, in a very general way, the complexity inherent in policy making and policy doing; at another level, we hope that some readers become as fascinated by policy making as we are and choose to do further reading in order to obtain a greater depth of knowledge.

Finally, as in all our work, we take full responsibility for what follows. That said, work such as this does not take place without the input of others and we'd like to take this opportunity to thank some of the people who helped us complete this book. First, we'd like to thank three cohorts of criminology and criminal justice students who, unknowingly, fed into the development of this project; we'd like then to thank the editorial team at Routledge for their help, advice and patience in the writing of this. Finally, we'd like to thank the people who have had to live with us as we completed this volume – never an easy task! Nick would like to thank Heather, Ben and Matthew for their continued support. Adrian would like to thank Quinnie for always being around.

1 Introduction

Origins of this book

As authors and academics we share a commitment to interdisciplinary working within the social sciences. Since we both started out in the field of social policy, perhaps this should be no surprise. One of the central features of social policy, in terms of both its application and its study, as far as we are concerned is that it is something of a magpie field (Blakemore, 1998), drawing evidence about the things that impact on welfare or well-being from every available source and as a result crossing a number of academic disciplines. Whilst this occasionally eclectic approach can be seen as a weakness at times, we strongly believe that being able to draw from a variety of sources allows a deeper understanding of social problems often in a more holistic way than unitary discipline pathways. It has provided us with the ability to teach and research in a number of areas over the years, including criminology and criminal justice studies. It was essentially as a result of our experience of teaching policy-related issues to criminology and criminal justice students that the idea for this book took shape.

Despite the reality that criminology, but more so criminal justice studies, is arguably a specific branch of social policy, in many areas and many programmes we found that the *process* of policy making is an underdeveloped aspect of the curriculum (and, as an aside, we would suggest it is a neglected aspect in some types of criminal justice and criminological research). The result of this fundamental lack of understanding about how policy is made, for whom, by whom and the constraints that policy makers and policy doers operate under, led otherwise perfectly able students to make unfounded criticisms of current arrangements and put forward unachievable utopian suggestions for policy advances. As Ismaili (2006: 255) points out:

> As the criminological subfield of crime policy leads more criminologists to engage in policy analysis, understanding the policy-making environment in all of its complexity becomes more central to criminology. This becomes an important step toward theorizing the policy process. To advance this enterprise, policy-oriented criminologists might look to theoretical and

conceptual frameworks that have established histories in the political and policy sciences.

It is in this spirit that we have tried to operate, though perhaps emphasising policy making as a process first and then applying criminal justice examples to illustrate its relevance. As governance and policy making has become increasingly driven by a desire for evidence, and this is shaping every area of public sector activity in the UK, understanding how policy is conceived, implemented and evaluated becomes ever more important.

What we have tried to do in this volume is speak across the boundaries of policy studies and analysis and criminal justice and criminology, with the aim of providing a basic introduction for students of criminal justice and criminology to the area of policy. Hopefully it will appeal to people with a general interest also, although as Waterstones – one of the major book retailers in the UK – was amongst the few places that escaped the attention of looters during the 2011 riots in cities across the UK, maybe this is a little too optimistic!

However, having taught criminology and criminal justice to undergraduate students, we are aware that in the main they seek to understand their chosen subject in terms of 'crime' and therefore expect the majority of information to be about 'crime'; if it is not, our experience is that they begin to complain that 'it's just not relevant'. To a degree we suppose this is true, but, sadly, it is a narrow conception of what the discipline is about. Nevertheless we have accepted this and, because of the need to be seen to be 'relevant', we have written the book with the assumption of little prior knowledge about policy making (or politics for that matter) and a recognition that for the majority of criminology and criminal justice undergraduate students there will be no need to understand the minutiae of the policy-making process; rather, a broad and general overview of the principles and practices will suffice. Thus, what follows is not a detailed policy-making book, and nor is it meant to be. It is a book that is intended to be an accompaniment to other areas of the discipline, one that allows students to appreciate that although they may disagree with any given policy, it has not suddenly appeared but is the product of a complex convergence of a number of factors and will take an equally complex approach to change it. In the final analysis we hope that this gives readers a starting point for developing their own interest and understanding of this vital and compelling aspect of social relations and interaction.

Structure of the book

In chapters 2 and 3 we have attempted to set the scene by focusing on the role of the state in policy making and introducing the reader to the centrality of political ideas. While policy is a universal activity that we all engage in – even deciding to make punctuality a personal guide to our behaviour in relation to others is to employ policy making – the criminal justice system in the UK is predominantly the responsibility of the state. At the time of writing the role of the private sector is under review, and the West Midlands and Surrey police services have caused consternation in some quarters by announcing that key aspects of their work will be put out to tender – including criminal investigations (http://www.dailymail.co.uk/debate/article-2110423/West-Midlands-Surrey-Police-privatisation-help-bobbies-beat.html). Nevertheless, while the balance may constantly shift in a mixed economy of provision, the reality is that the state will retain control of criminal justice for the foreseeable future.

Having made this observation, it begs several questions. What is the state? Is it simply what the central government does or decides? What role does local government play? And taking into account more recent developments, how will we, as citizens or subjects, play a role in our own governance? Whether this is part of a third way or as part of laying the foundations for a Big Society, such questions will become more pressing. The purpose of chapter 2 is to give the reader a brief introduction to policy making as a function of the state.

The third chapter moves away from grounded political realities to an exploration of the place of ideas in the formulation and implementation of policy. While Tony Blair and to an extent Gordon Brown and David Cameron, as successive prime ministers, have all expressed a desire to escape ideological constraints and instead concentrate on 'what works', it is our contention that this is not actually achievable and may even be disingenuous to suggest. Ideas are as central to policy making in contemporary society as they have always been and for those studying these issues for the first time it is imperative to understand this. All we can hope to do in this short book is to highlight the principal ideologies that retain their explanatory power and give the reader some stimulus to guide their own ideological adventures. When reviewing policy, and criminal justice policy in particular (Grimshaw, 2004), it is as well to keep in mind the question: in whose interests?

In chapter 4 we begin to think about the nature of social problems and more specifically the process of establishing what count as problems that are worthy of policy attention. This follows on from the ideology discussion very neatly because from our perspective identifying the motives for action is inherently about ideological matters. What is seen as a problem and acted upon and by the same token what is ignored are very much the products of the world views of policy actors. Again this runs counter to the dominant political discourse at present, but that is because in claiming ownership of common sense politicians and others can appear invulnerable to criticism. Who would dare argue against common sense or what is seen to work? As academics, students and citizens/subjects we must not allow that to happen. Without problems to overcome policy would seem to be unnecessary, but to seek to obscure the importance of ideas is itself an ideological sleight of hand. In short, pretending to transcend ideology becomes its own ideological position. Chapter 5 places this into a criminal justice context by introducing the key players and agencies who bear responsibility for different aspects of policy. The information provided here is up-to-date at the time of writing but, just as with everything else involving policy, the personnel and processes change very quickly. Once you have the basic structure though, it is then far easier to negotiate this dynamic process.

Having set out the policy environment for criminal justice, we then – in chapter 6 – describe the process by which social problems are translated into meaningful action. Policy making is one thing but actually implementing that policy is another matter altogether, and the reader needs to understand what makes this translation possible and what serves to make this process difficult. The implementation gaps that policy makers are frequently faced with – that is the gap between what policy makers want to happen and what actually does happen – can often lead to policy 'failing' or at least not making the intended impact. There are all too often unintended consequences of policy making. Not the least of these numerous barriers are the so-called 'street level bureaucrats' (Lipsky, 1980). If we are going to make policy directing the beat priorities of police officers, then we are to some extent limited by the willingness to comply of the targets of our intended outcomes. Some public servants have a great deal of discretion and are powerful enough to frustrate the aims of policy. In reviewing this, we first set out the ideal circumstances for policy making as exemplified by leading commentators, then use this framework to show how the actual rarely conforms to the ideal. In philosophical terms the 'ought' of a given situation does not often reflect the 'is' …

An important factor in modern policy making in the UK is the way in which public sector institutions co-operate with each other and with organisations and actors across other sectors. Joint working is therefore the subject of chapter 7. If responding to problems from a unilateral standpoint is difficult enough, then adding in the complexities of working with other agencies and organisations provides an extra dimension. Here we set out the distinctions between multi-agency, interagency and joint working. While this is a huge and expanding area of social scientific writing and research, the chapter walks the reader through the historical origins of joint working and the practical, potential and significant problems of making and delivering policy in such a context.

Chapter 8 rounds up the policy-making process by looking at what happens once a policy is designed and implemented. Without evaluating how a policy has worked (or not) there would be no way of revising and refining it or, if necessary, abandoning it and changing direction. Of course, the latter is rare because of the investment in political credibility, time and resources that are expended in policy making. As we said above, as evidence has taken on more significance, evaluation and audit have also seen more emphasis. Even in academic circles this is having a major impact. Once upon a time conducting research and producing journal papers and books were considered the ultimate goal of academic work; now we are being asked to evidence the 'impact' of our work. While this is potentially a positive thing, there is suspicion that it is as tokenistic as the previous priorities. Regardless of this, evidence is imperative, and understanding how it is gathered and interpreted needs to be addressed.

The final substantive chapter takes equal opportunities in the criminal justice context as its subject. What we have tried to do is to bring the material produced in the preceding chapters together – as far as possible – and use equal opportunities in policing as a specific case study. The interest for us lies in the reality that equal opportunities has been an ongoing problem for the police service, with anxieties about the ability to understand and respond to the policing needs of diverse communities. In 1999 the police service was labelled as institutionally racist by the Macpherson Report, and it would be hard to think of a larger problem for any agency to overcome. We discuss the way in which the problem was conceived, the process by which policy advanced and its outcomes as far as they can be judged to date. The magnitude of the change required underlines the importance of ideology but perhaps the gap between stated objectives and real policy intentions. The magnitude of change required is so significant that it may be impossible to achieve without a thorough restructuring of policing. As far as policy goes, this is as difficult as it gets.

A parting shot

Policy is an inescapable part of modern living, and while it may seem tiresome at times, one of the ways to make it more interesting is to engage with it as a living, breathing entity. If you can achieve this, you will begin to understand the complexity of policy making as well as the manner in which policy makers at all levels (supra-national, state level, local and even within your own university) have huge impacts on what becomes possible. The excitement and the possibilities inherent in policy making have been beautifully articulated by Kingdon (1984: 128):

> Many people have proposals they would like to see considered seriously, alternatives they would like to see become part of the set from which choices are eventually made. They try out their ideas on others in the policy community. Some proposals are rapidly discarded as somehow kooky; others are taken more seriously and survive, perhaps in some altered form. But in the policy primeval soup, quite a wide range of ideas is possible and is considered to some extent. The range at this stage is considerably more inclusive than the set of alternatives that are actually weighed during a shorter period of final decision-making. Many, many things are possible here.

We hope that you come to find policy as fascinating as we do and that in some small way this book acts as a very small step in your future studies.

2 The role of the state in the policy-making process

Introduction

The starting point for this book is to examine 'the state'. This is an important launch pad for what comes later as 'the state' is often the bedrock for all types of policy-making organisations. It is also important in more practical terms as it provides us with a frame of reference: often in general conversation people will say 'such and such is an outrage, *they* should do something about it'. For example, during the riots which took place in the United Kingdom (UK) during the late summer of 2011 there were cries from all sections of society for something to be done – the common refrain was '*they* need to do something'. More often than not the '*they*' to which people refer is the state or state agencies providing services on behalf of the state; in the example of the riots it was the government directing the major state criminal justice agencies such as the police, courts and prisons to which people were referring. That this has been a long-standing feature of police–community relations can be seen in the commentary of Bittner (1974) who referred to policing matters as involving 'something which ought not to be happening, but about which someone ought to do something *now!*' (cited in Newburn and Reiner, 2007: 213). As such, the state has incredible importance in policy making and policy doing, two concepts and practices we will explore in the forthcoming chapters. However, it is important that you understand from the outset what is meant by 'the state' as it is a phrase that is often used without explanation but in reality is a complex and changing mixture of concepts and practice.

What you also need to understand is that, generally speaking, policy generated by the state takes precedence over all other forms of policy, and it is very nearly always the case that those who transgress against state policy will suffer some form of sanction, if they are caught. This may seem obvious but have you ever paused to consider how this comes about? Why do we allow the state to punish us if we break the law? Equally, policy made by the state should, in theory at least, be of benefit to all citizens, but is this really the case? If it is not, then in whose interest does the state operate? Remember our central question from the introduction: in whose interests? It is important that you have some understanding of these questions because their answers have a direct effect on the types of policy which will be made, the sections of society at which policy will be targeted and the manner in which such policy is implemented. This chapter provides some information about the state and the manner in which it operates, including the tools it has at its disposal, and concludes with some thoughts about power and the state.

'The state'

The best place to begin this section is to define what is meant by 'the state'. Whilst there are a number of definitions, they all have core elements in describing and defining what the state is. For our purposes, the definition of the state by Abercrombie *et al.* (1984: 241) is a good starting point. They define the state as:

> a set of institutions comprising the legislature, executive, central and local administration, judiciary, police and armed forces ... it acts as the institutional system of political domination and has a monopoly of the legitimate use of violence.

Thus, when we talk about 'the state' what we mean is an entity that is much more than simply the central 'government' in Westminster – it encompasses the bodies which form what is known as the political executive (parliament, local authorities and the political parties); it also includes the institutions which we can see as the machinery of government (departments and official organisations).

The term 'state' can also be used at a number of levels: supra-national (as in the case of the European Union), national (as in the case of the United Kingdom, UK) and more recently in the devolved institutions in Scotland, Wales and Northern Ireland, or locally (as in the case of Plymouth City Council). Flint (2006: 105) provides this useful conception of the multi-layered nature of 'the state':

> A state is the expression of government control over a piece of territory and its people. The geographic scope of governmental control exists in a series of nested scales. For example, the London Borough of Hackney is a scale of government nested within the Greater London Council, the United Kingdom and the European Union.

Power to make and implement policy is diffused within this nested system, with decision making and enforcement capabilities being spread across 'the nest' often according to a principle known as 'subsidiarity'. This is a term we will explore later.

The state also creates, retains and bestows on the government, and the machinery of government, the monopoly of the legitimate right to use violence to enforce its will. Again, this monopoly of violence is an important definitional and practical point. Put simply, it provides the state and state agents with the right, in certain circumstances, to use force, up to and including lethal force, not only against the external enemies of the state (for example foreign terrorists) but also against its own citizens. Again, it is important to note that the decision and the right to use force are applied on a sliding scale, with the local state having far less power to enforce its will by resort to force than the central state.

For our criminal justice-based policy purposes we need to begin to think about the state as being the government at central and local level, including those organised political parties that take part in the democratic process, as well as the institutions which implement state criminal justice policy, such as the police, prisons, the Crown Prosecution Service, courts and probation, as well as the increasing use of private companies that are contracted by the state to provide aspects of criminal justice policy. But the state moves beyond the organisations themselves: it also *becomes* the functions these organisations perform, because the organisations work on behalf of the state and for the state.

At this stage it may be easier to begin to understand this by looking at the manner in which state institutions working in the criminal justice sector make abstract concepts such as 'justice' manifest, or 'real'. For example, the police are a state institution that 'does' police work on behalf of the state. Depending on the nature of the state, this work ranges from providing a public presence (the bobby on the beat function), to keeping public order, to investigating serious crimes, to using armed force to address offending behaviour. Thus, one aspect of police work is to arrest and question suspects on behalf of the state; police keep the peace in the interests of and on behalf of the state. Equally, the court system is a state institution which turns the abstract concept of justice into a tangible outcome by deciding guilt and innocence, sentencing people and so on. This is important as in theory at least the work of the criminal justice system is done on behalf of the state and not on behalf of the organisations themselves. For example, some police officers may believe that we need to decriminalise cannabis and therefore stop arresting people for possession of that particular drug. However, until the state decriminalises cannabis, police officers, as agents of the state, are duty bound to keep arresting those in possession of cannabis and not allow their own beliefs to influence their actions (though, as we shall see, the role of discretion is hugely important in examining the policy-making and policy-implementing processes) (Lipsky, 2010).

Apart from the obvious elements of the state, some people see the media as part of the state inasmuch as it represents an 'establishment' which promotes and sustains a particular world view (Schlesinger, 1981). This became a very important topic during the invasion of Iraq with the development of 'embedded journalism', the location of journalists in military units theoretically to increase their access to 'live' events. This was interpreted as propaganda by many, rather than an enhancement of war-reporting, and there were even variations between the perceptions of the general populations of different countries (Donsbach *et al.*, 2005). More recent domestic events surrounding the now defunct *News of the World* have also made an impact on popular perceptions, with the suggestion that many state agents have had very close working relationships with the media; we will return to this in more detail in forthcoming chapters. The important point for you to note at this stage is that the state encompasses more than just 'the government'.

Finally, it might also be worthwhile to pause to consider how 'the state' shapes your identity and how others, especially from other nations, see you. Beyond the practical manifestation of state power, it can also be argued that 'the state', when linked to national identity, is an abstract concept which serves to promote a shared identity and fix normative ideals about what ought to be – consider the scenes at every World Cup or major sporting championship, be it football, rugby or cricket, and the fervour induced by supporting 'England' or 'Wales', 'Scotland' or 'Ireland', or in the case of the Olympics Great Britain. This connection arouses passionate responses; in responding to an article by Jim White (2012) about the value of having a multinational and multi-ethnic British team to contest the Olympics, a regular blogger on the *Telegraph* site said:

> Jim White praises the multi-ethnic composition of Britain's Olympic team in today's Telegraph (LINK), and this is my response:
>
> What this article reflects is state ideology (not coincidentally, the exact but equally extreme opposite of Nazi racial ideology) which denies, demonises and suppresses as 'racist' the natural ethnic basis of national identity, which the liberal (and not so liberal) Left has succeeded in imposing on all western democracies since the end of WW2. The NATION has been removed from what was supposed to be our 'nation state', leaving us with just a mercenary STATE, for which it is the 'colour of money' rather than the 'colour of someone's skin' (i.e. ethnicity) that counts. Just look at the role that money plays in sports (including the Olympics) nowadays!
>
> I no longer see Britain as my NATION, because it isn't one, and thus won't.
> (http://my.telegraph.co.uk/philosopherkin/tag/national-identity/)

Just as national events can appear to bring communities together in the perception of shared identities embodied in a state, they can clearly equally illuminate tensions and divisions. Arguably, managing this is a key function of the power of the state.

There are any numbers of ways for 'the state' to operate and to exercise its power. In Britain, we have a particular form of the state which is generally known as a 'Western liberal democracy' (WLD) and is one of about 40 similar liberal democracies in the world (Budge *et al.*, 1998: 4). Broadly speaking, WLDs are states which have regular elections enabling most citizens above a prescribed age to choose which political party (or parties) will form the government (local, national and, in the case of the member states of the EU, supra-national). All citizens over the prescribed age are able to vote in these elections (with a few exceptions in some cases). Importantly, WLDs guarantee citizens' rights which cannot be taken away without the agreement of the democratically elected government. As we will see below, theoretically, in WLDs power lies in the hands of all the electorate as the people both (s)elect and de-select the government.

Another important feature of WLDs is that the use of state violence enacted on its own citizens to enforce the will of the state is undertaken as a last resort and as such is rare (but not unknown). Note the reluctance of Theresa May, the Home Secretary at the time of the riots in 2011, to use the armed services to regain control of the areas affected. Generally, in WLDs governments make policy which is debated in and through the media. Although these debates can be fierce, they are generally peaceful. In some cases, demonstrations, usually in the form of protest marches, take place. Again, apart from a few cases, these are generally peaceful. Once these have been conducted, policy making and implementation usually continue, occasionally with some adjustments made in response to popular concerns. When WLDs do use violence on their citizens, it is usually undertaken by the police and not the military. However, it is important to note that some would argue that, given the concerns about global terrorism, state violence in WLDs is actually on the increase, and that this has impacted more severely on specific communities, Muslims in particular (Vertigans, 2010).

However, not all states operate in this manner. For example, many single-party states (sometimes referred to by the Western media as 'dictatorships') are not based on democratic principles as we know and understand them. In turn, it is not unusual for the rulers of such states to use oppression and violence in order to establish and maintain power over their citizens and remain in power until the state is changed via revolution, populist resistance or, in the case of Iraq, foreign governments creating regime change. Citizen-led change has been at the forefront of what is being called 'the Arab spring' across North Africa in 2011, where the death of Mohamed Bouazizi, a young man who set himself alight in response to the police seizing his vegetable cart, led to rioting by young Tunisians, which in turn has led to regime change and seemingly irresistible demands for reform in countries such as Egypt (see Blight *et al.*, 2011, for a useful and interesting timeline of events).

Equally, there are some examples of leaders failing to give up power even in the face of the democratic decisions of the people. As we write this chapter, the Ivory Coast is in turmoil because Laurence Gbagbo has refused to cede power and in the process has dissolved the government and the electoral commission in that country and effectively seized power. Alongside this, the winner of the election held late in 2010, Allassane Quattara, has also formed a government. At present the Ivory Coast has two governments, each trying to run the 'state'. This begs the question: which party has legitimacy and to whom do the people turn? Having raised this question, we will now move on to explore the nature of the relationship between people and the state.

The relationship between state and citizen in WLDs

This is a huge area of study and one that we have neither the space nor the need to explore fully (for those of you who wish to look at this further, Scott (1996: chapter 7) provides an interesting perspective of power from a sociological position). However, it is important that you have a basic understanding of this aspect of the state as it has a direct bearing on policy making and policy implementation. Hill (2005: 26, emphasis added) suggests that: 'The study of the policy process is *essentially the study of the exercise of power*, and cannot ... disregard ... questions about the sources and nature of that power.' This is an important point and the theme of power will continue throughout the remainder of this work. As noted above, in some forms of the state, state power can be, and often is, exercised through violence, fear and repression and in those cases the relationship between the state and citizen is one of domination and subordination. Thus, in most dictatorships, policy will be made for and by the dictator and the state machinery will be directed at the protection of the dictatorship at the expense of submitting to the will of the people. Whilst there is often pretence that the state is acting on behalf of its citizens, it is often the case that this is a thin, transparent veneer which neither the citizens nor the wider international community believe.

That is not the case, in theory at least, in WLDs as power lies in the hands of the electorate and the state is said to operate on behalf of the citizens and not for itself or for one section of society. That said, it might be useful to pause and reflect on how much influence you, your family or even your immediate neighbourhood have had on criminal justice policy in the course of your life time. In all probability your answer will be 'not much', yet the state and criminal justice policy and machinery are said to represent your interests and to be enacted in your name. What is happening here and what is the relationship between power, the state and the citizen? Who holds that power and how and for whose benefit is it exercised in the policy-making process? These are key questions about the nature of policy and have generated a wealth of debate and discussion. Below is a very brief overview of three key theories. For those of you who wish to explore this area in more depth, see Hill (2005: chapter 2) or Kavanagh *et al.* (2005: chapter 3).

Pluralist theories of the state

In its pure form, democracy is seen as requiring an active citizenship engaged with making day-to-day decisions about the running of the state. In this way the state becomes for and of the citizens. In a large and complex state such as Britain this is impossible – if we were all consulted on every aspect of the state's work in terms of its criminal justice policy, nothing would ever get done. Equally, the same applies for the local state: think of the place where you live. Would it be feasible for the local state to continually consult all citizens on each and every aspect of the work it carries out? Clearly not.

Democracy in large complex societies has thus become something more than the direct participation of all citizens in the state's activities. In practice the way that most WLDs work is that elections are held within a set period of time which is long enough to allow governments time to enact policy but short enough to allow meaningful change to take place if the citizens believe it is required. So, in the UK's case the citizens vote for a person and/or a political party who becomes their representative in a national parliament within a five year period of the previous election, with the same principle applying in most cases for a local assembly. These democratically elected representatives are then given a mandate – power – to make decisions on behalf of the citizens who elected them. As such, all citizens are entitled to contact their elected representative and to express their views on matters of the state. This elected representative joins others in some form of parliament or assembly where the business of the state is discussed and decisions are made.

In theory the result is that the will of the majority prevails in most instances, because there is a unified executive response to the will of the people. Periodically, there are elections where the citizens can get rid of their representative(s) if they feel that they are not doing a sufficiently good job. In this way power is said to be distributed evenly across the population as the majority of the adult population have the right to vote and an equal right to contact their elected representative.

In practice WLDs are not as simple as that. There are other influences on the state machinery, the majority of which are very well organised, often with resources such as personal contacts as well as money, and which we can term pressure or 'lobby' groups. These can include global corporations, trades unions, environmentalists, ethnic minorities, sexual minorities, pro and anti-smokers, consumers of welfare and so on. (Interestingly the media can also be seen to represent a specific interest group which calls into question its role as an arm of the state and indicates the complexity of the relationships and inter-relationships that constitute governing or governance; see Meer *et al.*, 2010.) These pressure groups seek to influence decisions, gain access to those with power and put pressure on governments at each stage of the policy process. As a result of wanting to remain in power, political parties begin a negotiation process with these groups. Thus, for some commentators, such as Macpherson (1980) and Galston (2002), WLDs are seen as being 'pluralist' inasmuch as power is diffused between politicians, the citizens and the various pressure groups, with no single group dominating the decisions of the state. If it is the case that WLDs are pluralist, then it can be said that they represent all citizens' interests. *The important point to emphasise here is that in theory no single group dominates the state and thus power is evenly distributed across all areas of society and all social groups.*

However, we need to issue a word of caution here. One of the key proponents of this theory, Dahl (1961), warns against thinking that in pluralist states power will be evenly distributed. Instead, at different times in the political and policy cycle the different interest groups will hold more or less power relative to the other groups. Thus, in every political cycle our interest will be represented to a greater or lesser extent at any given time. According to Galston (2005) – one of the keenest proponents of this perspective – the United States provides a good example of pluralism in operation because it combines political pluralism, value pluralism and expressive liberty (the social space which enables the public expression of different views and values). Pluralism as practised by the USA is encoded in a constitution and frames a citizenship defined by tolerance. In examining these claims, we need to review competing theories of the state.

Elite theories of the state

Abercrombie *et al.* (1984: 84) define an elite as 'a minority group which has power or influence over others and is recognised as being in some way superior ... even in nominally democratic societies and institutions'.

There are a number of elite theories but they all share a common thread – that of the existence of a superior and tightly knit group of people, who come together through a shared characteristic which can take the form of social background, membership of a profession or access to forms of power and control (the ownership of the media, for example) that enable them to take some measure of control over the state. This is justifiable in the eyes of certain commentators (ironically who themselves may be part of the elite) because some people are 'better' than others and contribute more to society than the 'common herd' (Henry III, 1994). The key point is that, even in WLDs, membership of elites is restricted, often undemocratic and very often hidden from the wider citizenry. As such, elites are predominantly unelected, often shadowy and, it is claimed, represent their needs over and above the needs of the general population. There are some obvious and visible elite groups which emerge and continue as a result of the role they hold in WLDs. Such groups are not elected but are simply given power as a result of their position within a key state agency. For example, judges, top military leaders, senior police officers and key civil servants exercise large amounts of power over the policy-making process but are in the main unelected. Depending on the level that they operate, this can be seen as a 'democratic deficit'; hence the desire by authors such as Lea (2000) to see more public involvement in areas like policing to reduce this perceived deficit, even challenging long-term problems such as racism (an issue we cover in more detail in chapter 9). Arguably, policy makers seek to close this deficit by plugging what they regard as an implementation gap, on the understanding that as elected representatives they embody the will of the people. Whether the implementation gap and the democratic deficit are synonymous though really depends on the perspective we adopt – with levels of trust in politicians at an all-time low (Seldon, 2010) clearly many feel that unelected public servants are better standard bearers of the 'will of the people'.

However, these people are visible and their rise to prominence is relatively transparent (the barriers that impact on the opportunities of certain groups in society will be explored in chapter 9) and can be followed via career progression. Moreover, in theory at least, it is possible for anyone to rise through these professions to become one of the elite whatever their original background. These cases apart, for some elite theorists there is an altogether more shadowy and questionable form of elite group. As we complete the writing of this book, the Coalition government headed by David Cameron is under pressure for 'entertaining' funders of the Conservative Party at 10 Downing Street and refusing to publish the guest lists. The fear is that the individuals involved are buying their way into influencing the shape of government policy (Hope and Hughes, 2012). On a global scale such groups provide the fuel for the work of political journalists such as John Pilger (2002), who has identified a small band of international capitalists as the 'New Rulers of the World'. On a much smaller scale in the UK, and which may relate to the Downing Street dinners, a great deal has been made of the continuing influence of Oxbridge (a term constructed by combining the names of Oxford and Cambridge universities) and public school educated elites in British politics – twenty-seven British prime ministers have graduated from Oxford, and another fourteen from Cambridge.

When you stop to think about this, the Oxbridge axis somewhat resembles a production line, where a handful of people are educated (and moulded?) by another handful of people, mostly sharing the same social and economic backgrounds and beliefs yet purporting to represent and understand all UK citizens. If this stance is adopted, the dominance of two elite universities over the British political system has serious implications for the perspectives and understandings brought to the leadership of the UK. Currently, two of the three leaders of the main political parties (David Cameron and Nick Clegg) are public school/Oxbridge educated, with several key colleagues also coming from the same social and educational background.

Why should this be a problem? The principal argument is that it works against the ideal of social mobility, that anyone from any background should be able to reach the higher echelons in society. The degree to which social mobility is a reality, or at least the extent to which social mobility operates, is a fiercely contested topic, with writers such as Peter Saunders claiming that the capacity for people to rise and fall in British society is perfectly attuned to the genetic and cultural virtues across different socio-economic classes or groupings (Saunders, 1989, 2010, 2011). According to the Organisation for Economic Co-operation and Development (OECD) such claims do not reflect the facts, as Britain has a poor record of social mobility when compared with similar WLDs. And maybe we should not be too surprised, as elites reputedly have the tendency to reproduce themselves and close off opportunities for other groups. But it also brings the whole idea of representativeness into question. As a commentator from the *Daily Mail* recently stated:

> For very few senior Tories come from a relatively poor background. And when ordinary families, already feeling the pinch as the economy slides back towards recession, are confronted with pictures of George Osborne

[the current Chancellor] on the Klosters ski slopes, they could be forgiven for wondering whether we really are all in this together.

(Sandbrook, 2011)

Sandbrook was actually pointing the finger at *all* political parties, and his view, a common one, is that elites do not understand the needs of a very diverse society; therefore, they are unable to effectively, and fairly, represent them.

(For those of you who are interested, all three party websites, www. conservatives.com, www.labour.org.uk, www.libdems.org.uk, have profiles of key members giving their backgrounds, including where they obtained their education. See this site for historical information: http://www.blanchflower. org/alumni/pm.html. It makes interesting reading for any concerned citizen, let alone for those who actually subscribe to elite theory.)

Scott (1991) argues that this elite educational background forms the basis for recruitment into the political ruling elite in Britain by providing a unifying force amongst top politicians. Interestingly Scott (1991) identifies one school – Eton – as being paramount in this process, continually providing key figures in the state and political machinery. It is worth noting that David Cameron is an ex-Etonian. *In this theory of the state, power is concentrated in the hands of a small elite group and the state is run to maintain the established status quo and to ensure that the small elite group retains power.*

Marxist theories of the state

Underpinning Marxist theories is the notion that in capitalist societies all aspects of state activity serve to support the interests of capitalism and seek to preserve this form of economic and social structure. The notion of elitism is also central to this particular theory of the state. It works because the capitalist state operates to mask the continued defence of capitalist interests. Because WLDs appear to be open to anyone and we all have the right to participate, the state appears to be class-neutral. However, this is an illusion because ultimately all state activity will support the capitalist class and ensure the domination and subjugation of the working classes. Thus, policy will always support the interests of business over the interests of the worker, and the separation of politics, state power and economics becomes impossible in practice (Milliband, 1972).

At this stage you need to be aware that this form of 'old fashioned' Marxism has been criticised for being too 'economically deterministic' and has largely been superseded by neo-Marxism, which especially draws on the work of Gramsci (1971) and Habermas (1976). Gramsci (1971) argued that the state comprises both political society – the army, the police, the legal system – and civil society – the church, the media, trades unions and political parties. Capitalism uses all of these state elements to secure its control of citizens. Gramsci (1971) called this 'hegemony'. Habermas (1976) suggested that capitalism has essentially bought off the workers with a supply of material goods, minimal welfare support (often paid for through taxation and other contributions) and trivial forms of entertainment. Many people would endorse this point; as we write this chapter, the euro is in turmoil; the banking system is unsafe; there are wars and revolutions in the Middle East. But the key points for popular discussion and media concern are *Strictly Come Dancing*, *X Factor*, *The Voice*, *Britain's Got Talent* and *I'm a Celebrity Get Me out of Here*! Some of these forms of light entertainment have even poked ironic fun at perhaps more cerebral commentaries on modern life – one can only imagine what George Orwell (2004) would make of the reality show *Big Brother*, for instance.

One of the ways in which the state operates through this process, according to neo-Marxists, is to create tensions and divisions between sections of the working classes in order to deflect attention away from the fundamental injustices on which capitalist society relies. For example, the way in which economic problems are laid at the door of immigrants (Paul, 1997), welfare scroungers (Garthwaite, 2011) and single mothers (Lewis, 1998) or the more recent blaming of public sector workers for the nation's economic ills. At times these 'problematic' social elements, excluding public sector workers, have been parcelled up in a discourse of the 'underclass', a class which exists below the respectable working class and threatens the very fabric of society (Murray, 1990a, 2001a). Even Marx acknowledged the existence of what he termed 'a lumpen proletariat' that had negative implications for class consciousness, unity and revolution. Neo-Marxists regard such efforts as propaganda, the means by which the inherent instability of capitalism and the injustices it creates can be for all intents and purposes concealed. Blame is placed on immigrants, not the mobility of capital and the economic benefits of conflict and warfare, welfare scroungers rather than corporate tax dodgers and growing inequalities, single mothers rather than the patriarchal relations constructed in the interests of capital. Quite literally, governments undertake an exercise in divide and rule. When discussing this and related matters or listening to others doing so, note how often they look sideways for the source of problems rather than upwards (metaphorically speaking). The degree to which you see the former would indicate the level of 'false consciousness' and the power of hegemonic forces according to neo-Marxist writers.

The key point to retain is that neo-Marxists have moved away from economic determinism to include a wide range of social and cultural influences in the maintenance of capitalist relations. However, the result is still the same – the domination of the state and citizens by the needs of the capitalist class and the ensured continuity of the capitalist social and economic system. *Within Marxist theories of the state, power is located in the hands of an elite group who seek to ensure the continuance of a form of economic and social structure where the needs of business and capital accumulation dominate the needs of the workforce.* A society that focuses on reduced productivity as a result of icy weather and snow, where workers would risk life and limb in going to work, might be seen as an example of this in operation.

Before ending this section of the chapter, it is important to note that the different models of the state we have described above do not exist in reality. Rather, they are what social scientists like to call 'ideal types' (Bradach and Eccles, 1989). That is, they are theoretical models that represent types of states in a pure form, rather than something which is tangible. A useful exercise at this stage of your understanding is to look at the British state through the lens each model provides; we suggest that you will see aspects of all three models.

We noted above that many aspects of 'the state' are abstract conceptual and theoretical constructs and that searching for tangible manifestations of these concepts can be a frustrating and ultimately fruitless pursuit. That said, we also noted that the manifestation of state power is a very real and often very visible thing, and it is to the manner in which state power manifests itself and the tools by which that power is applied that this chapter now turns.

Using power by 'doing' policy – the tools available to the state

In WLDs such as the UK state-instigated policy can be seen as a practical manifestation of the state trying to do something that benefits one social group or another (depending on your perspective) or at least respond to a problem; in short, policy can be seen to be the practical manifestation of the power to get things done (or arguably, just as importantly, to stop things happening, and we will be looking at this later on in the book). Thus, criminal justice policy becomes the state's response to 'the crime problem'. Although, as we shall see in the next chapter, there are many ways in which the state 'does' policy, the reality is that in WLDs the state is restricted to three core vehicles on which all policy will be based. These are:

- intervention based on legal regulation
- intervention based on the distribution of resources
- interventions designed to promote normative change.

There are the odd times where the state in WLDs will use overt physical force to impose its will, but whilst the state does have the option to use force, the use of force is generally seen as a last resort by WLD states (Lind, 1994). However, as we stated earlier, this may now be changing due to the real and perceived risks posed by global terrorism, and the death of Jean Charles de Menezes, a Brazilian man shot seven times in the head by the Metropolitan Police Service on the platform of Stockwell tube station, should be acknowledged here (for a full account of this tragic event see http://www.mpa.gov.uk/scrutinies/stockwell/ and http://www.justice4jean.com/). Based on those three key vehicles, we can see that, practically, all state policy will be implemented using at least one of the following methods.

The law

Defining the law is a complex and contentious activity; many different definitions exist and they also vary in different national contexts. Thus, for Gibbs (1968: 429):

> Debates over conceptions of law have an ancient history, and since the end of the eighteenth century they have become more intense. Given the fact that contemporary schools of thought in jurisprudence [legal philosophy] are distinguished first and foremost by the kind of definition of law advocated, it is difficult to understand Selznick's assertion that definitions of law 'are not really so various as is sometimes suggested'. To the contrary, one would be hard pressed to identify a more controversial issue in either jurisprudence or the sociology of law.

These have varied in length and complexity, from a system of rules (Dworkin, 1977) to:

> All the rules of conduct that have been approved by the government and which are in force over a certain territory and which must be obeyed by all persons on that territory (e.g. the 'laws' of Australia). Violation of these rules could lead to government action such as imprisonment or fine, or private action such as a legal judgement against the offender obtained by the person injured by the action prohibited by law. Synonymous to act or statute although in common usage, 'law' refers not only to legislation or statutes but also to the body of unwritten law in those states which recognise common law.
>
> (http://www.lawinfo.com/lawdictionary/dict-l.htm#L)

However we care to define it, the law is the bedrock of most state policy. For our purposes we will be concentrating on criminal law but, as we will see in the next category, the state can also use what is known as civil law. As such, both sets of law amount to a written code of conduct that is used to codify, prohibit or in some instances coerce certain types of behaviour through a system of threats and sanctions. For example, it is illegal to possess or supply certain types of drugs. Some people will never have anything to do with illicit drugs simply because they are against the law. In this instance it is nothing more than the threat of state sanction that affects behaviour. However, some people are willing to take the risk of sanctions and break the law relating to possession and supply of these substances. If they are then subsequently caught breaking drug laws, they will be punished in accordance with the seriousness of their actions, an outcome consistent with the 'just deserts' principle which guides most sentencing in the UK: personal possession will normally carry a lighter sentence than possession with intent to supply. However, if certain types of drug users are caught – most usually those with long-term and heavy use of a class A drug such as heroin or crack cocaine – then the law can be used to coerce them onto rehabilitation programmes, essentially forcing them into a behaviour change pattern (Bean, 2010). The law is the most commonly used of the three key policy vehicles in criminal justice policy.

Taxation and subsidies for individuals, social groups or organisations

In this example the government uses the power of taxation or subsidy to promote or reduce certain behaviours. In essence the government uses state power, often in the form of civil law, to manipulate certain aspects of economic, social or cultural behaviour, especially that which is seen to have large-scale positive or negative consequences for the population as a whole. For example, the state can use taxation to try to reduce potentially harmful behaviour. So, excessive alcohol consumption is generally seen to carry negative health implications and also has consequences for the criminal justice system, especially for the young. Alcohol is the subject of taxation and thus the raising of taxation levels on certain types of alcohol could lower levels of consumption and reduce the negative side effects of alcohol in the short and longer term. At present there are plans to introduce minimum unit pricing with the expressed intention of using price (taxation) to lower alcohol consumption. Similarly, the state can promote behaviour by subsidising it. For example, the state can promote the development of green policies by subsidising alternative forms of energy production, such as the recent subsidies to householders to install solar panels and then sell excess energy to the national grid (Gordon, 2001). This policy vehicle is rarely used directly in criminal justice policy, although the criminal justice system can benefit indirectly in some cases.

Trying to promote cultural and social change

Often the state seeks to promote a certain type of behaviour which will be based on an ideologically informed, normative ideal of what a 'good' citizen ought to be. However, whilst the state can pass laws, impose taxes and subsidise schemes to promote cultural change, it can and does also emphasise certain types of behaviour which it endorses and highlight certain behaviours which it sees as negative. For example, over the past thirty years the cultural practice of home ownership has become the norm for housing tenure in Britain, but until the 1980s home ownership was only one of a number of options.

Equally, we could look at Anti-social Behaviour Orders as the state promoting a certain type of behaviour, via the civil process in the first instance, in order to ensure that the state's version of 'good' behaviour is entrenched and promoted. The hope is that anti-social behaviour will decrease and therefore become less and less common, thus creating a social and cultural change. This type of approach is now becoming more common in criminal justice, where the law is being used to promote cultural change. For example, the banning of young people wearing hoodies from entering some shopping malls could be seen as the promotion of a normative ideal of what young people should be. Equally, the drink aware programme (http://www.drinkaware.co.uk/) and the 'Talk to Frank' programmes (http://www.talktofrank.com/) are state-sponsored schemes aimed at promoting cultural change through information campaigns.

All of the above are tangible manifestations of state power and demonstrate the pervasiveness of the state. To a large extent we, as citizens, are generally expected to adhere to the first two forms of state power: if we break the criminal law and get caught doing so, we will face some form of sanction which often will have negative consequences for a period of time. Equally, with taxation, the vast majority of the population are unable to avoid taxes (interestingly for proponents of elite theory, the very rich are often able to circumvent some forms of taxation and this has become more evident over the past few months) and we have to acquiesce to the state taking a chunk of our earnings. Finally, state-sponsored normative behaviour becomes established over time and is often used as the yardstick by which 'good citizens' are judged. Thus, over time and via a combination of all three policy vehicles, the state moulds behaviour to fit its aspirations as to what constitutes a 'good state'. The degree to which the concept and practice of 'good citizen' and 'good state' benefits all sections of society will depend on your perspective on the nature of the state.

Thinking about state power

It should be self-evident at this point that power and the state are intertwined and that the concept and practice of power are at the centre of policy making (Lukes, 2004). Power is about getting things done and as such is at the heart of creating and sustaining any form of society. For our purposes, criminal justice policy is clearly based on power as it retains the right to punish those who transgress and break the law. However, as we have attempted to do above, it is important that we try to identify where power lies and which groups wield power in the state as that will give us some indication of the purposes behind policy and allow us to see the winners and losers. There are some key questions about power that you may care to consider. For example:

- Is power always about force or can it stem from coercion and compliance?
- Is power an evil thing which always corrupts those that hold it, or does it allow us to get things done and thus progress as a society?
- Does the ownership of power by some people reduce the power of others?
- Does political power lie in the individual or the institution?
- Are power and authority different things?
- Does the state hold power as a matter of right or does it have to elicit that power from its citizens?

Clearly, these are points for you to consider and they are open to much debate: we do not expect you to have concrete answers at this stage. On the contrary, as you progress it may be that your ideas will shift and fluctuate as your reading expands and you access more information – be assured, this is perfectly normal! However, it is worth ending this section of the chapter with the following thoughts from Brown (1981: 192). According to Brown:

> Power is force, coercion and repression; it is the gun, the fist or the fine; it is the police officer's hand on your arm or the bullet hole in your head;
>
> Authority exists where power is used by supervisors with the consent of the subordinates; in these circumstances force will not be necessary although it will continue to exist as the ultimate sanction;
>
> Legitimacy is the process by which power becomes authority; but whether legitimacy is freely given or whether it is actively elicited by rulers is a critical issue.

Conclusion

This has been a very brief but necessary look at the theories of state. The key elements of this chapter are:

- The state is not the same as the government.
- The state is about power over citizens and power is the capacity to get things done which most of the time manifests itself through what we know as 'policy'.
- Theories of the state ask you to consider where power is held and in whose interests power is used.

These are important questions and concepts and, although not always at the forefront of discussions concerning policy and policy making, should nevertheless be considered when thinking about and analysing policy. The next chapter begins our journey away from the abstract and into the more tangible world of policy and politics, although we are not finished with abstract ideas as the link between the abstract and the real is inescapable.

Questions for consideration

1. What do you understand by the phrase 'Western liberal democracy' (WLD)? In what ways does state power in WLDs differ from state power in dictatorships?
2. Take some time to study recent government policy and actions around aspects of criminal justice. Using your knowledge, highlight which model of the state is visible within those actions.
3. Do elections give citizens a voice in shaping and controlling state power?

Selected further reading

Abercrombie, N., Hill, S. and Turner, B.S. (1984) *The Penguin Dictionary of Sociology* (2nd edn), Harmondsworth: Penguin.

Hill, M. (2005) *The Public Policy Process* (4th edn), Harlow: Pearson Education.

Kavanagh, D., Richards, D., Smith, M. and Geddes, A. (2005) *British Politics* (5th edn), Oxford: Oxford University Press.

3 Policy, politics and ideology

Introduction

A good starting point for this chapter would be to provide you with a definition of 'policy' in order that you can fully understand what it is you are studying. However, whilst many writers have tried to define the concept of 'policy', there is still a degree of ambiguity about what is meant by the term, and as a consequence there is a distinct lack of an agreed definition. This is partly because the concept and practice of policy are vast subjects and touch all aspects of our lives and partly because policy comes in many guises.

For example, if you are reading this as a university undergraduate student, you will probably have noticed that your university has formal policies on any number of things relating to your studies, such as hand-in dates, rules regarding late hand-in of course work and so on; some of the pubs and clubs in the towns or cities where you live have semi-formal door policies such as making decisions as to what is and what is not 'properly dressed'; you have your own personal, informal, set of policies concerning the way in which you balance your studies and your social life. Each one of those aspects of your student life can be seen as a 'policy', but all are vastly different in terms of how formal they are, how effectively they are implemented, how they impact upon your life and the sanctions you experience as a result of breaking the conditions of that policy.

Equally, the state has a number of equally complex policies that will affect your experience of higher education, although you may not be acutely aware of them (those of you who are paying the new fees most certainly will be!). Thus it becomes very difficult to provide an all-encompassing definition of exactly what constitutes a policy. Our approach both in the book and in our work in general has been to paraphrase Cunningham (1963: 229): policy is a bit like an elephant – you know one when you see it but describing one is difficult.

Beginning to understand criminal justice policy

If we are unable to provide an all-encompassing definition of what policy is, we can at least identify some key characteristics of policy. At its most basic form policy could be seen as containing some or all of the following:

- a principled stance
- a distinct and stated set of aims
- a course of action.

For our purposes these three basic characteristics will serve as our main framework for understanding and analysing criminal justice policy, but for a selection of more formal and somewhat fuller definitions of policy see Hill (2005: 6–7).

The majority of criminal justice interventions fall into what is known as 'public policy'. Public policy incorporates what the economists call a 'public good' which means that it is paid for by the state, is available to all and is non-excludable (Parsons, 1995: 10–12).

It is important to look at this in a little more detail as Parsons' definition contains an important aspect of policy that is central to criminal justice policy inasmuch as public policy is non-excludable. An example of the concept of non-excludable in action means that, to use an often repeated phrase, no one is above the law: whoever it is that is breaking the law, if they are caught they will be punished in the same way as everyone else. An example of this would be Princess Anne's £400 speeding fine in 2001.

Public policy can be defined as 'a prior statement of actions and commitments of a future *government* in respect of some area of activity' (Colebatch, 2002, *our emphasis*). Whilst the key policy characteristics remain the same (principles, aims, ultimate action), public policy is different from other forms of policy because it refers to policy made by governments and in England and Wales policy made by the state has supremacy over all other forms of policy (except some instances of policies that are made by the European Union and we will examine this in more detail later). Equally, it is important to remember that the state has legitimacy to enforce this supremacy. Thus, even if a bar owner has a business policy of knowingly selling alcohol to people under the age of 18, and under 18s have a personal policy of buying alcohol, the state policy of sales of alcohol to under 18s being illegal will force the bar owner to stop selling and prevent the under-age drinker from buying if the offence is detected. State policies should literally trump organisational and personal policies when conflict is recognised.

So far, we have tried to explain policy in abstract ways. However, our belief is that the best way to understand this complex area is to use a series of real world examples, and it is to this we now turn. We are using the example below to illustrate the manner in which the three basic components of policy – a principled stance, a distinct and stated set of aims, and a course of action – play out in real life.

The example we have chosen comes from the previous New Labour government's 'Updated Drug Strategy' written in 2004. The first point is to examine these three 'policy' statements relating to the manner in which the government of the time intended to deal with illicit drug use:

1. 'Prevent young people from becoming drug misusers' (Home Office, 2004).
2. 'Reduce the use of class A drugs and frequent use of any illicit drugs among all young people under the age of 25, especially by the most vulnerable young people' (Home Office, 2004).
3. 'Frequent use is defined as twice a month every month over a twelve month period ... success will be if self-reported use of class A drugs is lower in 2007/08 than it was in 2003/04 ... vulnerable young people will be taken to mean truants, school excludees, young offenders and those young people who are homeless ... responsibility for this will be shared by the Home Office and the Department of Education' (Home Office, 2004).

All three statements come from the same original source – a selection of the Home Office's drug strategy documents found on the website www.drugs. gov.uk – and all three relate to the manner in which the previous government intended to deal with illicit drug use. In their various ways all three can be regarded as 'policy'. However, they are also vastly different and their strength as examples is that they represent how 'policy' can differ depending on who it is aimed at. Thus these examples provide us with an insight into the range and diversity of statements and accompanying actions that can be considered policy and also the manner in which all three basic components of policy come together to form a 'policy' that can be subsequently turned into action.

If we examine each statement in turn, this becomes more apparent.

1. Prevent young people from becoming drug misusers

Policy statement 1 can be seen to be a general 'sound bite' formulation of policy so beloved of political leaders. Whilst it is a commendable aspiration and arguably represents the views of the majority of the UK population, if you pause to think about it there is little in the way of substance there. What it does, however, is to represent a principle that illicit drug use is wrong and needs to be controlled. While we would suggest that it is difficult to argue with the sentiment of the policy, if you reflect on this for a moment you will see that, arguably, it is not that much more than a statement of principle. It lacks much in the way of focus, it lacks any form of clarity and it certainly lacks specificity. It does not tell us who will be responsible for implementing the policy, nor does it provide any idea of a time frame according to which the policy will play out. However, despite the fact that it lacks clarity or specificity we would argue that it *is* a perfect example of governmental policy and is a central part of what at the time was a key strategic document in dealing with illicit drug use in England and Wales. If nothing else it can be seen to be 'policy' because it expresses the key principled stance – illicit drug use is wrong and as a democratically elected government with a mandate to power we intend to do something about it – on which the following two examples of policy are built.

As an important aside, you may also want to ask yourself why the emphasis is on the word 'misusers' and not simply 'users' – there is a subtle but very important difference between a drug user and a drug misuser. It is worth stating from the very start of this book that words are of great importance in policy statements and every word in a policy document is the subject of a great deal of scrutiny and thought. Very few words enter a policy document without their meaning being thoroughly explored.

Moving on to policy statement 2:

2. Reduce the use of class A drugs and frequent use of any illicit drugs among all young people under the age of 25, especially by the most vulnerable young people

Here we can see that this statement moves to clarify the principled stance expressed by policy statement 1 and is clearly a set of specific aims. It is more detailed than 1 and provides some specificity. For example, there is a sharper focus now on the type of drugs that will be targeted – class A drugs which include heroin, cocaine and crack cocaine – and to a degree we have an identifiable group on which to focus beyond the highly generic term 'young people'. Instead, policy statement 2 clearly specifies vulnerable young people and it is this group who have become the main target of the policy. Nevertheless, despite adding some degree of specificity the policy still remains vague. For example, who will be responsible for this? How will it be done? What will success look like? How will success be measured? What constitutes a 'vulnerable young person'? What constitutes misuse? However, in spite of this vagueness we would suggest that policy statement 2 moves beyond the principled stance outlined in 1 and supplies us with the second component part of policy: a distinct and stated set of aims.

Moving to the final statement, policy statement 3:

3. Frequent use is defined as twice a month every month over a twelve month period ... success will be if self-reported use of class A drugs is lower in 2007/08 than it was in 2003/04 ... vulnerable young people will be taken to mean truants, school excludees, young offenders and those young people who are homeless ... responsibility for this will be shared by the Home Office and the Department of Education

Here we begin to move further away from the abstract and more opaque nature of policy statements and to see the manner in which the principles and aims will be translated into tangible action. Policy statement 3 provides even more detail and clarity and provides us with a clear and stated course of action. It tells us exactly what the policy will be seeking to achieve, identifies our priority targets, provides us with a time frame and informs us of the manner in which success is to be gauged. It defines all our concepts such as misuse and vulnerable young people. It tells us how we will measure success.

It also provides us with information on which government departments will be responsible for delivering the policy. In fact, it provides us with an operational framework that can be observed, measured and evaluated for success. It does not tell us *exactly* how this will be done, however, which is all too often a key failing in the move between policy formulation and policy implementation, a point to which we will return in a later chapter.

In the real world of policy implementation there will be policy statements 4, 5 and probably 6, 7 and 8 as the policy becomes more refined and moves to turn policy into practice and the course of action becomes more and more specific. (In fact, if you are interested, closer examination of the www.drugs.gov.uk website will provide more refined examples of policy that detail exactly how the Home Office and Department of Education will turn the broad aim of 'Preventing young people from becoming drug misusers' into reality.)

The object of this short excursion through some actual policy documents is to demonstrate to you that 'policy' can move from being a broad statement of principle (policy statement 1) to a set of aims (policy statement 2) through to a detailed and precise course of action (policy statement 3). It has been included because it moves our written work on policy making away from a discussion of what is and what is not policy in abstract terms by using examples from 'real' criminal justice policy; it allows you to see how the three key component parts of policy merge together to turn an idea or principle into a tangible and measurable course of action. Doing this to live policy is a useful exercise and you are urged to do it yourself with contemporary criminal justice policies. Dissecting policies in this way is good practice and, in terms of honing your understanding, time well spent.

Using a 'real world' example also serves to introduce you to what is known as 'the policy process' (Colebatch, 2002). This relates to the way in which an ideology, or a world view on what is right and wrong, is turned from a political principle (as expressed in policy statement 1) into a set of aims (as expressed in policy statement 2) and on into a course of action designed to address a 'problem' (as expressed in policy statement 3). However, that is the subject matter for another chapter. This chapter now turns to ideology and politics and the manner in which these two interrelated concepts are at the heart of most state policies, and indeed most policy activity *per se*.

Ideology, politics and the British social and political landscape since 1945

If policy originates from a set of principles, then our first question must be to ask from where do such principles emerge? In the world of policy as made by states and governments the answer to that question is from the expansive and sometimes murky pool that is political ideology. Abercrombie *et al.* (1984: 118) note that 'ideology is one of the most debated concepts in sociology'. This book is not the place to enter into that debate; we simply do not have the space here to do the subject justice – see Eagleton (2007) for a thoroughgoing exploration that places different ideologies in their historical context. So for our purposes, when we refer to 'ideology', we have in mind the following definition, which has its roots in American political science:

> a tightly knit body of beliefs organised around a few central values
>
> (Abercrombie *et al.*, 1984: 118)

It is worth considering this definition in tandem with Easton's statement that:

> Policy is a web of decisions and action which allocate values
>
> (Easton, 1953, cited in Hill, 1997)

If that is the case, then clearly policy will reflect the ideological values of the policy maker, which will, in turn, impact on the way in which abstract policy is turned into practice. *This is an important point and one to which we will return in the following chapters.*

Indeed, it is generally agreed that our ideology presents us with a world view and carries with it a set of normative behaviours (that is what ought to be rather than what is) which can then be applied to all aspects of social life. Political ideology is not fixed – it can and does change: witness the demise of classic Marxism and the rise of neo-Marxism as discussed in the previous chapter. It can also emerge from the combination of different individual elements, such as the creation of the New Right ideology by weaving together neo-conservative and neo-liberal components (King, 1987). Consequently, as policy is related to ideology, it follows that shifts in ideology and mergers of ideological elements will have a profound effect on the direction and shape of policy.

Clearly any policy which fits Parsons' (1995) definition of public policy, rendering the impact of such policy non-excludable (meaning that every citizen is subject to it), becomes an important and powerful political tool because it affords politicians the opportunity to try to shape the way society operates to reflect their own ideology. A key aspect of ideology and its success in shaping behaviour is often the way in which it becomes invisible and unconsciously imbibed as 'common sense'. So important is making a value-laden set of ideas seem like 'common sense' that it is seen by some as the goal of the ideologue (Morley and Chen, 1996). As we shall see, this sometimes means actively denying the existence of an ideology to promote the idea that a projected political plan is simply a matter of 'realism', pragmatism or just plain 'common sense'.

For instance, note how many times the present British Prime Minister, David Cameron, uses the phrases 'sensible decision' or 'sensible policy' in his speeches. Whilst this phrase sounds neutral enough, those who look deeper will see that a decision or policy is only 'sensible' if one agrees with the basic principled stance and ideology that underpin it. What Cameron, amongst many others, is actually doing is to attempt to dress his particular ideology up so that it becomes hidden and is disguised as 'common sense', despite the fact that in reality all decisions are based on a discernible ideology. As time passes, ideology will change and what is now seen as 'sensible' will be seen for what it is, a standpoint, and another form of ideology will emerge which in turn will be seen as 'sensible'. To make these points clearer we will now move to demonstrate how ideology changes over time and how those changes affect policy, which, in turn, seeks to change the nature of the political and social worlds.

A brief history of changes to British society since 1945

In Britain there was a significant shift in the political landscape from around 1979 (though the extent of the shift is itself subject to our ideological perspective) with the election of the first Thatcher government, and it is important that you are aware of the nature of these changes in order to understand our present system, contemporary policies and the manner in which these policies are implemented. The changing nature of the British political landscape is covered in detail in any number of politics, policy and social history books and we note some of them below in the 'Selected further reading' section at the end of the chapter.

However, the roots of 'Thatcherism' lie much deeper than the 1970s and our starting points reflect this. We start our review of British political and social history at the end of the Second World War in 1945. Britain and her allies were victorious in the war but paid a high price in terms of lost human life, finances and infrastructural damage. Once the fighting ended, what remained of the United Kingdom was a country that had large sections of most urban areas either partly or in some cases wholly destroyed due to continuous high intensity German bombing raids. It also had a shortage of adult males due to high mortality rates amongst the armed forces and was in serious debt because of the high cost of financing the war. In short, it was a nation that was in need of rebuilding, a task which posed a set of serious economic, social and, arguably toughest of all, political problems (Glennerster, 2006).

However, amongst the politicians and policy makers of the time there was what is known as 'cross party consensus', which revolved around the prin-cipled stance that the rebuilding of Britain should include not just a physical rebuilding of the infrastructure and economic base but also the construction of a more just and equitable social structure. As a result, more than ever before in British history, the state took responsibility for addressing some of the key aspects of social structure which were seen to be at the heart of social inequality in pre-war Britain. This principled stance and accompanying set of stated aims focused on what Beveridge had identified as the 'five giants' of social inequality – want, disease, ignorance, idleness and squalor (Beveridge, 1942).

These five giants cover the key social requirements of a decent wage, freedom from preventable and treatable illness, access to a good education system, access to meaningful employment, and decent housing. Broadly speaking, it was felt that these five aspects of social life were too important to be left to the vagaries of the market and that the state had a responsibility to meet all these basic needs by owning buildings, employing workers and running the organisations via a set of public administrators. Policy was to be formulated by a tripartite (three way) system which included government, the trades union movement and business leaders. Middlemas (1979) referred to this as a 'continuous contract', with economic interests driving governmental priorities, and orchestrating the needs of these key social actors became the work of government.

Accordingly, the state set about devising policies around this principled stance. It adopted an economic policy known as Keynesian macroeconomics, the intellectual product of John Maynard Keynes, which placed creating demand at the heart of government economic policy in order that it could generate enough tax revenue to fund the ambitious rebuilding projects (Heilbroner, 1998). From this perspective it was better to fill huge holes with money and have people dig it up than to allow high levels of unemployment. As a result the state, and not the private sector, took responsibility for funding (through high levels of income tax and corporate tax) and building a wave of new hospitals, schools, municipal buildings and houses, thus providing employment, either directly in the case of nurses, doctors, teachers, social workers, bureaucrats and administrators or often indirectly in the case of contractors, for a huge swathe of the population. The often quoted aim was to create a state-delivered 'cradle to grave' welfare state (Timmins, 2001) which would be funded by high levels of taxation gathered from full employment – unemployment in this schema should never fall below 3 per cent of the working-age population (defined, it must be said, in predominantly male terms). In effect, what this created was a monopoly of provision (that is only one provider of any good or service) of welfare by the state. Put simply, for the majority of the population the only form of social welfare – health, education, housing – which was available to them was that supplied by the state.

It is also worth noting that optimism for this project was so high that there was a belief that the 'five giants' that had hitherto led to entrenched social problems could be 'cured', never to return. Whilst there was some disagreement over aspects of this social and political settlement, the dominant political perspective was that this was the best way to run Britain. In fact, there was a widespread belief at the time that ideology was dead, that ideas were irrelevant in the face of this new pragmatic reality. What emerged was an emphasis on administration and planning. Authors like Mitrany (1934) believed that the explicit withering of political ideas is always an essential component of any attempt to engage in practical planning. Equally there were commentators who called the whole basis of consensus into question (Pimlott, 1988; Harrison, 1999). Of course, as with so many claims of this type, it was as much about perception as it was a true reflection of reality. Nevertheless, it was a very important and widely shared perception, which has been described as 'Butskellism', a term created out of pressing together the names of two chancellors of the time: Hugh Gaitskell (for Labour) and Rab Butler (for the Conservatives) (Plant, 1985).

The problem with shared perceptions is that they are subject to challenge, and this was no less true for the belief that the era of consensus was eternal and spelt the end for political ideas than for any other perception. It is beyond the scope of this chapter to explore in detail why the crumbling of the practice and perception of consensus occurred, but inevitably the post-war consensus did start to crumble from the beginning of the 1970s and by the end of the 1970s there was a deep political division about the future direction of British public policy. As a nation, Britain was still plagued by deep social divisions, poor housing, low wages, ill health and, importantly for the purposes of this book, rising crime levels.

The 1960s saw a 'rediscovery of poverty' by sociologists Abel-Smith and Townsend working from within the London School of Economics, and this was a very demoralising realisation (Beresford and Croft, 1995). By the time we approached the end of the 1970s it appeared to some that the very fabric of British society was under threat (Pemberton, 2000). Briefly, that threat was seen to come from two areas: internally via militant trades unions holding too much power and a disillusioned workforce and externally via changing global economic circumstances. It was argued that Britain's economy suffered from an amalgamation of internal factors – falling production, rising wages and escalating inflation – and changes to the global economy – the emergence of new alternative economies, rising oil prices and ever more enterprising competitors – which led to a perceived decline in all aspects of public life. To put it bluntly, Britain was generally perceived both at home and abroad as being a failing nation; the Conservatives in opposition during the 1970s repeatedly referred to Britain as 'the sick man of Europe' (Reddaway, 2007).

Questions were quite naturally posed in an attempt to ascertain why this was the case and as always these questions spawned new ideas and new approaches. For some, much of the blame for Britain's relative decline fell on the welfare state, with the claim being made that the 'cradle to grave' welfare system had created a dependency culture that stifled ambition and negated the need to work hard (Self, 1993). Why should people work hard when, at one level, their earnings were so heavily taxed and when, at another level, substantial rewards were obtainable without working? The principle of 'less eligibility' that had historically steered welfare support (that income support should always be less than the lowest available wage) had been compromised, it was argued in some quarters. Margaret Thatcher took the helm of the Conservative Party in 1975 and was influenced by key figures including Keith Joseph (who in turn had been influenced by 'neo-liberal' economists such as Hayek and Friedman). Ideologues such as Joseph used the difficult social, economic and political circumstances of the period to craft a new ideology for the political right. This ideology, whose principles and adherents are often referred to as 'the New Right', brought together neo-liberals who regarded freedom in the marketplace as fundamental with neo-conservatives who prioritised tradition, order and morality (George and Wilding, 1994). Although there were areas of policy that could not be reconciled by the two ideological components, at the beginning the solution was simple: reduce the involvement the state had in people's lives and encourage them to take greater responsibility for most of the crucial social and economic aspects of their lives (Forbes and Ames, 2012). Once this ideological perspective took root, the policy solution to the ideologically defined problem was to reduce the amount of influence the state had on the lives of the general population and to increase personal responsibility. The 'nanny state' had to be challenged.

The election of the Conservatives under Thatcher in 1979 demonstrated which way the British people wanted to go. One of her early targets in a widely quoted speech was the very notion of trying to gain a consensus in politics; she said:

> To me consensus seems to be the process of abandoning all beliefs, principles, values and policies in search of something in which no one believes, but to which no one objects—the process of avoiding the very issues that have to be solved, merely because you cannot get agreement on the way ahead. What great cause would have been fought and won under the banner 'I stand for consensus'?
>
> (http://online.wsj.com/article/SB100014240527487
> 04471504574445072280951620.html)

Essentially, her election signalled a move away from reliance on the state to a greater reliance on the individual and the market to provide welfare above that of a very basic level of social support (Alcock, 1990). This is variously described as a residual or minimal welfare state. Accompanying this were questions about the manner in which those who worked in and ran the welfare state dominated policy making and the nature of the services they delivered. There were two basic but fundamental criticisms of state welfare and of state employees:

- First, welfare services, including local government, were run for the benefit of those that worked in them and not for their clients.
- Second, state provision was in most cases inferior to that provided by the market.

The solution offered by the Thatcher-led Conservative Party was to 'roll back the state', that is to reduce the amount of influence and input the state had on people's lives (Le Grand, 1997) and to introduce the market into those areas of provision that had been monopolised by state provision since 1945. The result of that would be to allow more private companies to provide welfare services, thus introducing competition through privatisation and ultimately ending the state monopoly (Gamble, 1988; Wolfe, 1991). Thus, a new ideology first challenged and then supplanted the Beveridge-inspired approach to the key areas of social provision. The New Right displaced the Middle Way if we want to retain our focus on ideologies (George and Wilding, 1994).

The subsequent four decades have witnessed the cementing of the market-focused, so-called 'Thatcherite' ideology, to the point where the supremacy of the market has become the dominant ideology and has effected a fundamental change to the political and social landscape. Examples of this abound: the reliance on the state to provide housing has almost vanished; educational provision free at the point of delivery stops at 18; there has been an expansion of private healthcare, a process which may reach its apex with the current Health and Social Care Bill; state pension provision is seen as only a basic measure and in need of topping up. We are used to mixing state, third-sector, informal (care provided by friends and family) and private provision to ensure that all our welfare and social needs are met. This is sometimes known as 'the mixed economy' approach to welfare (Osborne, 1997). Equally, there has been a shift in the manner in which the country and state organisations are run. Gone is the old tripartite arrangement, with the trades unions being ever more marginalised in policy making. Even the Labour Party has sought to distance itself from union influence. Interest groups such as the Green Movement have arguably replaced the trades union movement as the voice of the people in government. In state organisations there is an emphasis on managerialism (more on this in another chapter) as opposed to the old-style bureaucratic administration and control. Those in receipt of state services are seen as customers not clients. The spirit of this perspective is exemplified in this quotation by the former president of the United States, George W. Bush:

> I'm absolutely opposed to a national health care plan. I don't want the federal government making decisions for consumers or for providers. I trust people; I don't trust the federal government. I don't want the federal government making decisions on behalf of everybody.
>
> (St Louis Debate, 17 October 2004, cited in Botti and Iyengar, 2006: 24)

This has become a major source of debate in the UK also, with prominent writers such as Le Grand (2007) arguing that choice can be both a means and a mechanism for ensuring optimal welfare outcomes, making the most of what the market gets right and harnessing it for the sake of improving the quality of public sector provision and policy making. Others believe that choice is not an appropriate value for public services:

> Consumer choice is an inadequate mechanism for empowering public service users. People want to feel confidence in services which are intended to meet their welfare needs. But it is no longer possible or acceptable to conceive of such confidence as based in unquestioning trust of service professionals.
>
> (Barnes and Prior, 1996: 51)

From this perspective, and even according to President Bush, one of the central problems is 'trust'. In this country the lack of trust in state provision has been propagated by the same forces that have sought to promote choice. Despite the problems associated with consumerism as a factor in the relations of social welfare it is manifest throughout the public sector.

If you are aged under thirty-five, all these things probably seem 'normal' to you, what Mr Cameron may call 'sensible decisions' – but they are, in fact, recent developments in the manner in which we address social problems, and that normalcy has been created by a shift in political ideology. What is important is that you realise that to effect these changes successive governments since the 1979 election have used the three basic component parts of policy that we outlined at the start of this chapter. That is, they will have used:

- a principled stance, based in this instance in the belief (or ideology) that the market is on the whole 'better' at providing services than the state;
- a set of stated aims, which, for illustrative purposes, would mean expanding the process of marketisation into the manner in which criminal justice provision is run;
- followed by a course of action, which, again for illustrative purposes, could be seen to be allowing private companies to run state prisons (Perrone and Pratt, 2003) and, increasingly, take control of other areas of criminal justice policy such as investigating crime scenes.

All of these changes to the manner in which Britain is run stem directly from a change in the ideology of those that run the country. This brief excursion into recent British social, economic and political history is designed to alert you to the fact that ideology can and does change and that, if a new ideology becomes dominant, the changes wrought by that new ideology can shape public attitudes and government policy for decades. However, what is equally certain is that, given a similar situation where negative external factors and negative internal factors collide to cause a decline, fresh questions will be asked and this provides the context in which a new ideology will assuredly take root. Even where the death of ideology is announced, the reality is that it is simply concealed beneath references to pragmatism or 'common sense' (Barton and Johns, 2005).

Conclusion

By now it is hopefully clear to you that providing an all-encompassing definition of policy is difficult as policy has many different guises. Nevertheless, despite the slippery nature of policy as a concept, it should be equally clear that state policy is undoubtedly a central aspect of our day-to-day lives – every aspect of what we do is covered by some form of state policy. You need only reflect on this for a moment to identify numerous ways in which state policy has impacted on you and your loved ones in the past week, even on the very day that you are sitting reading this book. If you are reading it for the purposes of formal study, then arguably the state is setting the context of your reading.

From your reading of the second section of the chapter it should also be clear that policy is based on ideology and values, and we would argue that it is *always* the case that policy reflects the ideology and values of the policy maker (but not always the values of the person charged with implementing the policy, a point we will return to later). At this concluding stage it is worth reminding ourselves of our two main definitions of what policy is:

> a tightly knit body of beliefs organised around a few central values
> (Abercrombie *et al.*, 1984: 118)

> a web of decisions and action which allocate values
> (Easton, 1953, cited in Hill, 1997)

Thus we contend that in the policy-making arena it is impossible to separate policy from ideology, and that the starting point of any policy analysis should be to look at the principle on which the policy is based as that will reflect the ideology and values of the policy maker. We would accept that ideology is only a factor and that ideologies can be composites, even a pick-and-mix, of different ideas and values; nonetheless, it will always be present in one form or another.

What do you need to take from this chapter? At the very least you should understand the three basic key characteristics of policy, which are:

- a principled stance
- a distinct and stated set of aims
- a course of action.

You should also register the fact that any 'policy' will have at least one of those characteristics within it.

Secondly, you should understand the meaning of the concept of 'public policy' and the fact that public policy takes precedence over other types of policy and importantly is non-excludable, meaning in theory at least that no one person can opt out of state policy. Even where people flout policy, when the conflict is publicised, something will be done even if it remains at the level of rhetoric. Thirdly, you should understand that most public policy is informed by an ideology. Broadly speaking, the current dominant ideology in British politics favours a 'third way' approach with shared responsibility for social provision as a mixture of personal responsibility, state provision and private organisational provision. All aspects of social provision (including criminal justice provision) can be provided by a mixed-economy approach, with private companies, third-sector organisations and state agencies working together – and increasingly a stronger involvement of the informal sector. It should be underlined, however, that this third way has been variously interpreted as a sophisticated means of concealing class allegiances favouring the elite (Jordan, 2001; Hall, 2003; Levitas, 2004), the renewal of social democracy (Giddens, 1998, 2000) and a thin cloak for traditional socialism (Dell, 2000; Coates, 2003). However we view this issue, at the time of writing this ideology is seemingly under challenge from the Conservative–Liberal Democrat alliance as it struggles to come to terms with powerful external and internal forces challenging the economic and social fabric of British society, a struggle that has seen Prime Minister David Cameron refuse to sign a treaty that has led to the isolation of Britain in the European Union. Being the self-proclaimed 'heir to Blair' apparently has its drawbacks and it will be fascinating to see the consequences of this unfold over the next few years.

Fourthly, you should begin to realise that ideologically and value-informed public policy is a powerful political tool which can and does shape the nature of society. Thus ideology, politics and policy are almost inseparable, especially in the policy-making phase. Put simply, policy will reflect the ideology of whichever political party happens to be in charge of any particular country at any given time. Changes in political leadership will inevitably lead to a change in policy focus, although it can also work in reverse and a political leader can shift perspectives when necessary.

This chapter has covered a great deal of ground and as a result has sacrificed detail for breadth. However, we make no apologies for that as the rationale for the chapter was to make you aware of the basic arguments and points around what is a hugely complex but extremely fascinating and consequently well-covered area. There is a wealth of political, economic, sociological and history-based textbooks and other sources which you can use to add some more meat to the bones of the debate we have provided above. That said, it is important that you remain aware of these basic principles and debates as they are visible in all aspects of policy and we will return to them in the ensuing chapters.

This chapter and the previous one have located policy making in the criminal justice system within the larger macroeconomic, political and philosophical realms. However, from here the book now moves to explore the meso and micro levels of policy making and policy doing. The next chapter looks at the important area of how decisions are made and how this impacts on what is and what is not considered a matter for 'policy'.

Questions for consideration

1. Consider your own ideological perspective: what is it? How would you describe yourself in ideological terms?
2. Could you identify three or four key principles that would inform your approach to forming criminal justice policy?
3. We noted that there are three key components to policy. Using government websites, select a current criminal justice policy document and try to identify each component part within that document.
4. Using your knowledge of criminal justice policy, could you identify the ideological perspective at the heart of contemporary criminal justice policy?

Selected further reading

Hill, M. (2005) *The Public Policy Process* (4th edn), Harlow: Pearson Education.
King, D. (1987) *The New Right: Politics, Markets, and Citizenship*, London: Macmillan.
Ling, T. (1998) *The British State since 1945: An Introduction*, Cambridge: Polity.
Parsons, W. (1995) *Public Policy: An Introduction to the Theory and Practice of Policy Analysis*, Cheltenham: Edward Elgar.
For an introduction to the notion of citizenship at the heart of the Beveridge Report (1942), see: http://www.nationalarchives.gov.uk/pathways/citizenship/brave_new_world/welfare.htm.

4   Decision making and agenda setting
Choosing what is and what is not 'policy'

Introduction

The previous chapter highlighted the role that politics and ideology have in policy making. It is important that you recognise this as from here onwards it will be a taken-for-granted assumption that at least some aspects of all policy reflect the ideology of the *policy makers*. However, as we also noted, their motivating ideological beliefs – a key ingredient – may not be shared by the policy implementers – the people that actually 'do' policy on the ground. This is important and it will be covered in detail in a later chapter. However, in this chapter we begin to move farther away from abstract concepts and begin to address some of the more tangible problems that face policy makers. Specifically, having discussed the role of the state, the nature of policy and the importance of ideology in policy making, this chapter examines the manner in which choices are made about which aspects of social life become worthy of policy. However, that seemingly simple task is in fact a complex one that involves the underlying political and philosophical ideologies and values of the policy makers.

For example, have you ever stopped to think how a social event or a piece of social action and interaction becomes worthy of having a state policy built around it? If not, then do not berate yourself, it is all too easy to let these things drift by unnoticed; hopefully we have helped to stimulate your interest and to ruin your comfortable lives in the same way that ours were ruined! But this is an important question because policy does not simply materialise: it is very often a planned and debated part of the state's business. Similarly, once a policy area has been identified and defined, how do we then go on to making policy and deciding exactly what will be done and how it will be delivered? Again, this might sound easy but it is fraught with problems and obstacles.

This chapter reviews some of the key points relating to this policy dilemma. It begins by looking at the manner in which policy is defined and the impact the process of 'defining' has on the nature of the 'problem'. As stated in the previous chapter, our perspective shapes our interpretation and our response. The chapter then moves on to provide a brief overview of political decision making and, importantly, non-decision making. This may sound like nonsense at this stage but trust us, it will begin to make sense as you read on. It then reviews the two main models of policy making – rational scientific policy making and incremental muddling through.

Defining 'problems' and politicising policy

Essentially, much criminal justice policy is made, or has been made in the past, as a response to a crime or social order-related problem – in our case a problem involving a criminal or anti-social act and/or what to do regarding the victims or perpetrator of a criminal act. A very simple way of understanding this process would be to see it in terms of a social event being defined as a social problem, leading to the design and subsequent implementation of a policy. Using that lens, we can begin to construct a useful scenario to illustrate our point:

Table 4.1

Social event	Problem	Policy
Young people 'hanging around' in public space after dark	Rise in anti-social behaviour	Anti-social Behaviour Orders

In the above example, let us imagine that a group of young people are using a public area in a city centre that has steps, rails and slopes as an ad hoc skateboard park, from around 6 p.m. until around 9.30 p.m. on week-day nights. Whilst the social event – young people hanging around and ska-teboarding – will be a tangible observable phenomenon, there will undoubt-edly be plenty of scope for disagreement about the nature of what is happening. It may become the case that groups of young people using relatively empty public space in a manner beyond that which it was designed for is defined by a combination of residents, the police and the local authority as a problem. Politically, once something has been defined as a 'problem', there is pressure to act: we do not elect politicians to do nothing and thus they are almost obliged to do something or at the very least be seen to be doing some-thing, which may seem ironic given the lack of trust many politicians themselves have in the state they are charged with overseeing (see the views of George W. Bush in the previous chapter). However, experience teaches us that once something has been defined as a 'problem', there is a very good chance that there will be conflicting opinions as to the nature of that 'problem'. Once this dis-agreement occurs (often based on ideological grounds), there will be debate as to the final shape of the response or, in the context of this book, the policy.

This is because whilst the social event is more often than not visible and can therefore be 'proven' in the shape of empirical evidence or the lived realities of the population, the nature of the problem and the shape of the response (that is, the policy) will be at least in part determined by the ideological and political values of the individuals and the political parties that are engaged in finding a solution to the perceived problem. In the above example, the perspective has been adopted that the problem lies with the young people and their presence in the city centre coupled with the unauthorised use of public space for skateboarding. This is either fuelling a rise in anti-social behaviour or is the actual manifestation of it. As a consequence of adopting this perspective, the 'solution' is to use formal social control mechanisms and agencies of the criminal justice system to change the young people's behaviour and/or remove them from that space.

But this stance is based partly on an ideological view of the role of social space and perceptions of the motives and behaviour of groups of young people. It is only one perspective and does not represent the only solution. Perhaps the best way to understand that is to re-visit our model above. Looked at from a different ideological or political perspective, our policy-making model could look like this:

Table 4.2

Social event	Problem	Policy
Young people 'hanging around' in public space after dark	Lack of facilities for young people	Rise in funding for youth work

If we look at the two approaches above, the social event remains the same but the perception of what the problem is and how best to solve the problem is completely different. In many respects, we can suggest that the manner in which the problem is defined sets the nature of the problem itself. Thus, if we add some more flesh to our skeleton social event, we could envisage a scenario where a group of young people hang around after dark in a public space and indulge in skateboarding, BMX–ing and generally hanging out. Because it is in a city centre and after 6.30 p.m. the area is devoid of the workers and shoppers that populate the space from 9.00 a.m. until 6.00 p.m. and thus is relatively empty. The young people are using the space and the urban landscape as arenas in which to practise and perform tricks and stunts on their bikes and skateboards.

However, some sections of society and some political groups will see this unauthorised use of public space as a threat and the actions of the young people as 'anti-social'. As a result the 'problem' will be 'criminalised' and the solution, or policy, will be criminal justice-led, and so 'doing' the policy will involve the police, police community support officers and perhaps the courts and the probation service combining their resources to eradicate the 'problem'. However, other social and political groups will see the 'problem' as 'social' and the response or policy would then be more welfare-based. In this scenario, 'doing' the policy will involve youth services and perhaps youth outreach workers, possibly operating from subsidised facilities to support and otherwise occupy the time of the 'problematic' youths in question. As a result of the decision-making process regarding what exactly the problem *is* in our scenario, different social agencies will be mobilised and the young people will be viewed either as a 'threat' or as a 'client group' with unfulfilled needs.

The above example is hypothetical but we are sure that if you look at the archives of your local newspaper, you will find a real life story which has many similarities. The purpose of including the vignette is to get you thinking about the multiple ways in which a social event can be viewed, and also to get you to consider the impact of ideology and political perspective on defining and then 'solving' social problems. In our example, we only provided two perspectives to the imaginary problem; in reality there would have been a range of perspectives and possible solutions.

This diversity in approaching problem definition and agenda setting is neatly summarised by returning yet again to Easton, who suggested that the best way in which to see policy is to view it as:

> a web of decisions and action which allocate values.
>
> (Easton, 1953, cited in Hill, 1997)

In this quotation, it is clear that Easton sees policy making as being fundamentally informed by the values (or if you prefer the ideology) of the policy maker. As a result, it is based on a normative assumption about the way society *ought* to work. Thus, Easton is making a claim that all policy is aimed at promoting a particular form of social action and that any decisions made regarding policy will be made in such a way that they reflect the values of the policy maker.

This has been underlined by the work of the American political scientist Murray Edelman in his seminal book *The Politics of Misinformation* (2001). His take on defining social problems adds a slightly different dimension that transcends 'interpretation'. Using a symbolic interactionist frame of reference – the idea that we construct social meanings through interaction – Edelman suggested political elites, the principal policy makers we have been discussing, deliberately 'mis-define' problems in order to deflect attention away from real social, economic and political problems. The concept he created to make sense of this was 'misidentification'. Using our existing formula, the definition process would look like this:

Table 4.3

Social event	Problem	Policy
Young people 'hanging around' in public space after dark	Preventing recognition of the lack of facilities	Anti-social Behaviour Orders

Here the problem is that an unwillingness to redistribute resources from the social and economic elites to the wider community prevents young people from having sufficient facilities to socialise and practise their skateboarding skills. This in turn creates a different problem for the political elite, which is the need to reframe the social event in such a way as to have the wider community accept the misidentification – that young people are causing a problem through their anti-social behaviour. In a sense the problem shifts in location, personnel and sequence in and through the definitional process. We will pick up on these different understandings of defining problems as the chapter and the book progresses, but first there is another aspect of decision making we need to consider – the decision not to act or to deny the existence of problems altogether.

A brief word on non-decision making and denying problems

Rather than engaging in the whole process of definition, it can be the case that it is in the best interests of the policy maker that social events do not become a 'problem' at all, thus requiring no action to be taken. Before moving on to examine how policy might be made, it is worth taking a small diversion to look at what policy analysts call 'non-decision making' or 'denying problems' (for a full discussion see Dorey, 2005: Ch. 2). Put very simply, some social events, or aspects of social events, will almost never be seen as a problem because these events are either politically or socially unpalatable for the majority of the population or they go against the dominant political paradigm and thus threaten the ideology or principled stance of the policy maker.

For example, the sexual and physical abuse of children is seen as a serious crime in Britain and one that taxes the criminal justice system. In turn, much is made of the criminal activities of so-called predatory paedophiles by politicians (Victor, 1998) and the media (Critcher, 2003; Williams-Thomas, 2010). When politicians and the media talk of paedophiles, they tend to refer to, or imply, either the threat of violent actions of total strangers towards children or the longer-term infiltration of the child's world by people (men in particular) who are not members of the child's immediate family (BBC News, 2011b). The 'threat' is said to come from these predators inasmuch as they infiltrate the child's world, either at random by means of force or over time by means of grooming, with the express intention of sexually abusing the child. Whilst there can be little doubt that the actions of these two groups of abusers do pose a threat, without doubt and by a large margin the greatest and most pressing threat to children comes from people known to the children.

The specific threat posed by known adults and family members has been acknowledged since at least the mid-to-late 1970s (Helfer and Kempe, 1976) and most commentators who currently study child abuse in depth now agree that children are much more likely to be abused by an immediate family member or close relative (Cawson *et al.*, 2000; Royal College of Psychiatrists (RCP), 2010). As the RCP suggests: 'It is quite unusual for strangers to be involved.' One consequence of this is that the bulk of child abuse often remains unreported and undetected (Gilbert *et al.*, 2009) whilst the rarer and more 'spectacular' form of abuse regularly makes headlines.

This observable social action creates a problem for politicians and policy makers in Britain inasmuch as the 'family' (which is explicitly and implicitly defined as a cohabiting male and female couple with the infamous 2.4 children) is sold to the British public as the optimum child-rearing vehicle, and it is generally agreed that it is this form of domestic social union that ought to dominate British society. Indeed, many social problems that are caused by young people are seen to be partially attributable to the lack of a stable family background (Barry, 2005). Moreover, some authors such as Charles Murray – a neo-conservative American sociologist – see this lack of stable families and absence of male role models as a key component in the existence of a deviant underclass (Murray, 1990b, 1999, 2001b). As a result of this normative assumption that traditional nuclear families represent the optimum family structure, any undermining of the view of the family as the male/female cohabiting couple being the 'best' and 'safest' environment in which to raise children becomes politically and socially unpalatable, despite the fact that most abused children are abused within the family setting and by immediate family members.

Thus in this instance, if we return to our formula above, child abuse may look like this:

Table 4.4

Social event	Problem	Policy
Child abuse	Intra-familial behaviour	Increased familial surveillance

This is because the tangible social event – the abuse of children – is identified by empirical evidence as most likely to occur within a family setting and result from inappropriate inter-familial behaviour. As such, the 'problem' could be defined as 'the family' itself and any subsequent solution (the policy) would need to be aimed at the family. This could include higher levels of surveillance of the manner in which all children were treated in all families and could be delivered by, for example, random spot checks by social workers and medical professionals on the physical and psychological well-being of children, or the perpetual surveillance offered by CCTV installed in the home reminiscent of Orwell's VidScreen.

In the face of the prevailing evidence, successive governments have tried to reinforce the conventional family model and the relationships it presupposes with a range of different policy measures (Barlow and Duncan, 2000; for a fuller discussion of the history of attempts to shape families, and particularly mothers, by the state see David, 1983 and 1985). The New Labour government that preceded the current Coalition, with its declared intention to more effectively balance rights with responsibilities, was extremely active in the area of family policy (Finch, 2004). Supporting families was seen as coded language for imposing middle-class values on working-class families. Indeed, the government were accused of generalising family policy from their own particular experiences: 'the aim of New Labour's re-socialisation programme is to make all parents into clones of Tony and Cheri Blair' (Gewirtz, 2001: 366). A wide range of advice was laid at the feet of parents to help them improve their performance, and there were proposals to extend health visiting roles to monitor and assist with the requisite skills (Gillies, 2005). Where parents refused to take up their responsibilities, there were tough sanctions, not least the criminalisaton of parents for the truancy of their children from school. In 2008 alone 9,506 people were taken to court for not ensuring the attendance of their children, though in spite of this absenteeism continued to rise (Clark, 2010). Despite these interventions into family life though, actually sending professionals regularly into the home to oversee parenting first-hand – other than the limited proposals around health visiting – was never even contemplated, let alone the routine surveillance of family life.

We imagine that such an authoritarian policy sounds absurd to you – 'not sensible' in current political parlance – and you can think of all sorts of responses as to why the state should not be allowed to adopt such an approach, as can we. These would include human rights, the sanctity of the private space, the requirement of privacy and abuse of state power. Nevertheless, the fact remains that child abuse most often takes place within the family and we do not have a system or policy in place to prevent it from happening; rather we simply react to events once the abuse has been uncovered or reported. An associated problem is that some women defined as the main care-giver in UK society (itself a major problem from a feminist perspective, Charles, 2000) and therefore above suspicion have remained invisible as paedophiles. That is until fairly recently, largely as a result of highly publicised cases (http://www.channel4.com/programmes/breaking-a-female-paedophile-ring/episode-guide/series-1/episode-1). Any meaningful prevention of child abuse perpetrated by immediate family members is impossible under our current political, legal and social configurations because it challenges so many of the key principles that underpin contemporary British society and social relations. This is because our policy response to the problem of child abuse is constrained and shaped by ideology, and associated political and social mores.

We could equally look at the social system and its effect on people. For example, capitalism is an inherently unequal social system and creates a wide variety of experiences in terms of income and wealth – some people are phenomenally rich and others are very poor and the gap between rich and poor is at its largest for at least a hundred years (Dorling, 2010). Marxists especially would argue that poverty causes many social problems – indeed much social research indicates that the poorest members of British society suffer the worst health, under-achieve educationally, have the worst diets, suffer higher levels of crime victimisation compared to other socio-economic groups and are over-represented in the ever expanding prison population (Wilkinson and Pickett, 2009). Given that, it might be the case that the majority of social problems could

be addressed by a vigorous and wide-reaching income redistribution programme, a massive increase in social spending and huge investments in poor
areas. Politically, this will not happen in Britain in the foreseeable future
because the dominant political ideology is vigorously opposed to old-school
socialist projects and is similarly opposed to the high rates of direct taxation
needed to fund income redistribution (Edelman, 2001).

It is possible to argue that the current policy of reducing public spending
and emphasising welfare benefit fraud whilst refusing to address tax evasion
by the very rich is evidence of just that. According to the Public and Commercial Services Union, £120 billion is lost to the UK exchequer each year
through tax evasion and the failure of the state to collect it; in comparison,
the amount of money lost through benefit fraud amounts to less than 1 per cent
of the lost amount of tax (http://www.pcs.org.uk/en/campaigns/campaign-
resources/there-is-an-alternative-the-case-against-cuts-in-public-spending.cfm#
Tax_justice).

Those are just two of any number of examples where 'non-decision making'
or 'problem denying' practices take place. In effect, governments can and do
set the agenda and decide which 'issues' or events to turn into problems worthy
of a response. Those of a cynical persuasion would suggest that political agenda
setting is done in order that politicians can claim to be 'doing something' and
that issues only become problems if politicians think they can devise a policy
to solve the problem in a manner which fits and adheres to an underlying
ideology or political philosophy, or, in Edelman's frame of reference, to deflect
attention away from the genuine source of problems.

Therefore we reiterate the point that it is important that we see policy as the
pursuit of political and ideological goals. These goals are determined and
influenced by a combination of philosophical and political values and require
the use of political power to shape society to reflect that ideology. In theory,
therefore, policy should be a purposive set of actions all of which are aimed at
achieving the stated goals of policy and thus making ideology and values
'real' inasmuch as they are reflected in the policy outcomes. In short, the
policy-making process should be a rational, objective and scientific process
which has a clear and repetitive cycle of decisions and actions. This approach
to policy making has been defined and discussed by a number of political
theorists, and it is to this theory that the chapter now turns.

Policy: objective, scientific and rational?

If we take the view that policy making is objective and goal driven, then it
follows that the policy-making process is a logical and cyclical series of events
where policy makers identify a problem, compile a comprehensive list of
solutions and resources and make an objective (thus value-free) decision
about the course of action to take. Once the policy is in place, it needs to be
evaluated to ensure that the goals of the policy are being met and, if necessary,
the original policy can be re-formulated to take into account the findings of

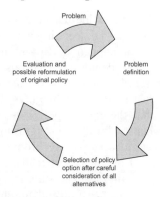

Figure 4.1 The policy cycle

the evaluation. The diagram above (Figure 4.1) provides a visual account of this process.

Colebatch (1998) argues that within the rational model of policy making there are three component parts to policy making that will be visible throughout the cycle. These are:

Coherence

This assumes that all the bits of action fit together to form a whole system or approach. This coherence is driven and steered by the nature of the desired goals. Another way to look at it would be to suggest that a policy goal which seeks to reduce the extent of illicit drug taking in Britain will only work if all the elements feed into and reflect the desired goal. Even more pro-blematically in the current policy-making environment, coherence has to be achieved across different aspects of criminal justice policy areas. The Minister for Policing and Criminal Justice in the current Coalition, Nick Herbert, in an early speech to the Policy Exchange in 2010 related the complexity of his new brief:

> Three years ago I wrote 'Policing for the People', the Conservative Party's radical agenda to bring accountability to police forces. I followed this with 'Prisons with a Purpose', with no less radical proposals to re-cast the penal system and reduce re-offending. Now I find myself charged by the Prime Minister to support Theresa May at the Home Office and Ken Clarke at the Ministry of Justice in driving these plans forward, reforming criminal justice policy, and attempting to ensure a coherent approach between the two departments. I am not sure whether I am a poacher turned gamekeeper, or a reform recidivist.
>
> (http://www.homeoffice.gov.uk/media-centre/speeches/
> nick-herbert-policy-exchange)

This shows the continuance of the 'holistic' approach to policy championed by New Labour, and so coherence has become increasingly important and complicated in a modern policy-making environment.

Hierarchy

The assumption here is that someone at the top is giving orders which are carried out by those below them or, as Colebatch (1998: 4) puts it, that there is: 'Authoritative determination of what will be done in some particular area' (Colebatch, 1998: 4). This is critical and in some respects is related to the practice of policy implementation which we will look at in detail in another chapter. However, at this stage it is clear that all policy needs someone at the top to instigate it and to ensure that it is carried through.

Instrumentality

This aspect asks the very important questions concerning whether the policy is related to particular purposes where there are clear policy objectives or goals. In other words, does the policy work and is it doing what it was intended to do? At this stage, we can say policy is made, and thus needs to be understood, in terms of problems and solutions. Accordingly, policy making requires three discrete elements:

- a mechanism to ensure coherence across the whole policy area
- a 'central nervous system' to ensure compliance across the whole organisation
- a need to fit and promote the overall aim or goal of the policy area.

If we take the example of equal opportunities as a key area for all public sector agencies, we can see how this works. A police service will have an equal opportunities and diversity policy that will, presumably, fit with the aims and objectives of the service. Certainly it has to demonstrate that it is complying with the law, and in doing so employing people without engaging in any unfair discrimination. For instance, looking randomly at the British Transport Police equal opportunities policy, we can see that it identifies the existence of its policy and sets out its responsibilities under legislation on its website (https://www.btprecruitment.com/btpr20068525315.asp). In order to oversee this policy the Human Resources Department with a dedicated Diversity Team take responsibility, thus providing the central mechanism for ensuring coherence and compliance, and the central nervous system would include the many support groups that have been set up to champion the cause of particular equality strands, for instance:

- the British Association for Women in Policing
- the Christian Police Association
- the Disability Equality Support Association

- the Gay Police Association
- LINK (Lesbian, Gay, Bisexual and Transgender)
- SAME (Support Association for Minority Ethnic Staff)
- the Women's Development Forum
- the Women's Support Forum.

This is not an exhaustive list, but it gives us a general idea of the reach and scope of the 'nerves' that help to keep the equal opportunities policy on track, along with the direction given by the Diversity Team. Of course without examining the policy and its context specifically we cannot comment on its efficacy, but what we can say is that the essential ingredients seem to be in place. We will come back to equal opportunities in chapter 9, but for now there are other critical things we need to address.

Essentially, there are a number of problems with this perspective on policy making, the main one being that it ignores the impact of ideology and politics – 'the allocation of values' that Easton referred to and that we have discussed above. It also ignores the non-decision making or denying problems models discussed above, as in some situations solutions will not be considered because they are politically or ideologically sensitive. Finally, it denies the complex reality of the political situations. It may be impossible to consider all the alternatives, or it may be the case that there is a policy option which will address the problem but cannot be resourced in time to be implemented. As such, the rational model can be criticised for not being fully aware of the influences of time, political necessity and the limitations of resources, be that defined as time, money or personnel.

Unsurprisingly, this perspective on policy making has been the subject of some criticism (Lindblom, 1959; Schneider, 1997; Parsons, 2002) and as a result a number of alternative perspectives have emerged, one of which sees policy making as little more than a process of 'muddling through' and it is to this perspective that we now turn.

Policy: complex, pragmatic and status quo maintaining?

Arguably, as we noted above, the rational model excludes the 'political' and real world elements from the policy-making process. Policy can alternatively be seen as something much more political (political with both a small and large 'P'), self-serving, sometimes corrupt and corrupting and *always* pragmatic. If we take this approach to our understanding of policy making, there are three elements that we need to be aware of, as one, some or all of the following three elements will be visible in policy and policy making.

Symbolism

At the most basic level it can be argued that we elect politicians to 'do things' and, in turn, politicians like to be seen to be 'doing things'. If you pause to consider some recent events, such as the riots in the late summer of 2011, you will see that some sections of the population questioned the fact that many of our political leaders were on holiday at the time of the riots and issued calls for them to return in order 'to take control of the situation' (Sparrow, 2011). Indeed Boris Johnson, who returned from his holiday in North America, faced angry crowds at Clapham Junction: 'When asked by one angry resident why he had not come home from his holiday earlier, the mayor replied: "I came as fast as I could."' (For the full video of this confrontation visit see: http://www.guardian.co.uk/politics/2011/aug/09/boris-johnson-clapham-junction-london-riots.)

Equally, by reacting to an event, politicians exude an aura of power in that they can claim to be 'addressing' the problem and as a result can be seen to be in control. Ironically, as stated before, this can even mean consciously undermining their own role as stewards of a state that cannot be trusted. Thus, politicians, whether at national, regional or local level, are expected to react once a social event has become problematised and, accompanying that, politicians are actually keen to visibly and verbally react as it gives the impression that they are in control, and, just like justice, control is as much about being seen to exist as actually existing (Weir and Beetham, 1999).

If we adopt this approach, we can see the making of policy as simply a symbolic exercise. By that we mean that in reality the chances that the policy will have a major impact on the problem is small, but by instigating a policy it symbolises to us that our political leaders are in control and able to shape and respond to social, economic and political events. For example, there have been several major Acts of Parliament passed in the last decade aimed at 'solving' the crime problem. Before we move on, it might be instructive to just pause and reflect on some of the more noteworthy of the measures that have been passed. One means of increasing crime is to look for it more assiduously, and we are certainly being watched more closely than ever before. By 2006 there were 4.2 million CCTV cameras in the UK, one for every 14 people (BBC News, 2006), and recently a Metropolitan Police Service report indicated that in one area of London where there are 1,000 cameras, the cameras themselves had helped to solve only one crime. This has occasioned an ongoing debate about the preventative impact of cameras set against the huge imposition on freedom. Doubts about the efficacy of CCTV on both reactive and proactive grounds appear to be well founded (see, for example, Webster, 2009).

Running parallel to the constant surveillance the UK general public is subjected to, it seems that the criminal justice system is designed to maximise the opportunities for individuals to 'fall foul' of it. People in England, Wales and Northern Ireland are held to be criminally responsible at the age of 10, maximising opportunities to criminalise the population. In most European countries responsibility is attributed to people aged between 14 and 16, and recent scientific research into the maturation of the brain has called the UK's position into question (Jha, 2011). Even attempts to bypass the criminal process have led some to enter the criminal justice system earlier and to accelerate individuals through it faster, chiefly as a result of the creation of Anti-social Behaviour Orders (Muncie, 2006).

The results of this short and selective list of the tough 'law and order' policies that have been introduced in the past 20 years can be illustrated in a number of ways. All of these are policies and all are aimed at preventing and reducing crime, yet despite this crime rates remain relatively high and relatively constant and, as we write, we are beginning to see a rise particularly in acquisitive crimes (http://www.ukcrimestats.com/). In concert with stubbornly constant crime rates, the UK boasts one of the highest prison populations in the Western world. In 2007 alone there were nine million people held in custody around the world, with the USA boasting just under a third of this total. Again the USA had the highest *per capita* custody rate at 714 incarcerations per 100,000 head of population, and while the UK is well below this, at 142 incarcerations per 100,000, it sits around the mid-point in the world rankings (Walmsley, 2007). Given the high costs of imprisonment and the limited impact it appears to have on crime, criminality and re-offending rates, some have referred to the situation in the UK as indicative of a 'penal crisis' (Cavadino and Dignan, 2007).

In truth, all politicians know that they cannot implement a policy that will have a major impact on crime in a Western liberal democractic (WLD) state, and 'criminal justice policy' is not about ending crime but is aimed at managing its consequences. However, if we adopt the perspective that policy making is largely symbolic, we could argue that by going through the very visible process of making criminal justice policy, and emphasising this by 'talking tough' about crime policy, politicians are able to give the impression of control while the reality is that much of the policy will have little or no impact on crime, criminals or victims, thus rendering much criminal justice policy largely symbolic.

A good example of this symbolism is the way in which the UK has approached the issue of prostitution. In the UK it is not currently illegal to sell sex but it is illegal to run a brothel or sell sex openly on the streets, which means that sex work is dangerous for the individuals who are involved and cannot be effectively 'managed'. It has been argued that unlike legislation in the Netherlands, where the perspectives of sex workers are taken on board and are used to guide policy, the UK relies on 'discourses' on public nuisance and moral order (Kantola and Squires, 2004). In addition there has been little consultation in the communities that are most affected by prostitution (Phoenix, 2009). The symbolic purpose of the prostitution legislation is to appear to be tough on public sex work, but in reality little is achieved except for further victimising what many see as the real victims of prostitution – the prostitutes themselves – by criminalising them and putting them in dangerous and uncontrolled situations. Underlying this symbolism is the power of certain groups to crystallise their views, norms and beliefs into legislation and policy, thus making them powerful and influential agents in the policy-making process, and it is on the issue of power that we now focus our attention.

Power

As Hill (1997) has noted, policy is about the exercise of power and power is a very intoxicating thing. Watching the demise of Margaret Thatcher as UK Prime Minister brought home in vivid terms the impact that losing such power could have on an individual. Policy can shape virtually every aspect of our lives, and it allows those that wield it the opportunity to see their own values and ideologies implemented across society. For example, it is arguable that, in terms of his domestic policy, Tony Blair's Christian values were clearly visible in his continued emphasis on morality, family, duty and respect. Equally, Gordon Brown's Scottish version of socialism is clear if one reads his speeches. The power to construct and implement policy provides all prime ministers and leading politicians with the opportunity to influence our lives.

One of the most interesting reviews of the concept of power and the manner in which it is employed is expressed in the wok of Stephen Lukes (2004). Lukes envisaged power as having 'three faces' and argued that to understand power we need to closely examine all of those three faces.

For Lukes, the first face of power is that which we can see; that is, the overt and often highly visible confrontations which take place. A quick and readily available example of this can be seen weekly at Prime Minister's Questions (although this could also be seen as a form of symbolism), where the Prime Minister and the leader of the opposition clash in a routinised and very stage-managed fashion. Another example drawn from a criminal justice perspective would be the police use of riot tactics to keep protesters at bay. The point is that here conflict is blatant and is concerned with ensuring that political and policy preferences are achieved and maintained.

The second face of power refers to areas of covert conflict. There is still a degree of conflict but it is at this level where conflict is expressed and power is wielded behind closed doors. Thus, it is in this realm where decisions can be made, but importantly it is also in this realm where 'non-decisions' are made: that is, issues are removed from or barred from ever appearing on the policy agenda. We know, for example, from the diaries and memoirs of ex-politicians that Cabinet meetings are often fraught and riven with conflict, yet these are seldom seen at the time by the general public except through leaks or journalistic suppositions.

The third face of power is the most deeply hidden and amounts to the power to shape and manipulate our desires. Here, Lukes argues that powerful bodies have the capacity to make people act against their own best interests and desire things that may actually be harmful to them. For example, the recent global economic problems have demonstrated that capitalism is an inherently divisive system that allows huge wealth to be accumulated and monopolised by a very small minority, while the pay and conditions of workers are steadily eroded at the same time as the support systems they rely on. Capitalism also exacts a huge toll on the environment, which threatens the future of even those who gain the most in status and wealth. Yet, through the skilful manipulation of systems like the media and religion, the capitalist ideology dominates politics and policy making with little in the way of organised opposition despite the misery and suffering it imposes on millions of people across the globe.

Incremental pragmatism

This refers to the fact that in many policy scenarios it is the case that very little that is different can be done due to political and organisational constraints. Policy makers seldom have a clean sheet on which to work and they become constrained by past policy and existing processes and organisations. In turn, this means that any policy changes will be small and often a compromise between what policy makers *want* to do and what they *can* actually do. To give an example: if we look at the police in terms of their ability to prevent crime, we could argue that the police are a failing organisation and we need something new to take the place of police forces that constantly fail to reduce or prevent crime. Marches and demonstrations have been organised around the world with this objective, with some people in San Francisco calling for the police to be disbanded because they are not needed. (Put 'Disband the police We don't need you in our streets – protest march in San Francisco' into the search box on youtube to watch a short clip of this event.) Even if we had some sympathy with these sentiments, how could we conceivably do that?

The answer is that we cannot in the short to medium term and we are stuck with the police as they currently exist and policing as it is currently practised and understood because the alternative is to work towards shutting down the existing police forces, devising and equipping new ones, setting new goals, and so on and so on, whilst at the same time allowing the existing police to continue through the period of transition. How could we recruit new police officers with the required levels of knowledge and training? How could we pay for a new organisation whilst continuing to fund the old? How could we ensure a smooth transfer of power? The answer to all those questions is that we probably could not and as a result police reforms are necessarily small scale and happen within the existing frameworks. The same is true across the whole of the criminal justice system; the ghosts of criminal justice past will continue to influence its present and future incarnations.

Conclusion

This chapter has covered a lot of ground and introduced you to some necessarily complex and contested concepts. There are no right or wrong answers here but by way of conclusion it is worth noting the following points:

- Defining problems is a political process, and some problems may be deliberately 'mis-identified'.
- Non-decision making or the denying of problems happens on a daily basis.

- Policy will always reflect the values of the policy makers.
- Policy will not be made if it is deemed politically dangerous or unpopular. This rule increases in strength the closer we come to a general election.
- Policy makers are nearly always constrained by existing policy and processes and existing organisational structures.
- Sometimes overtly, but always implicitly, ideology and power are integral components of policy and policy making.
- At best, policy making is a quasi-scientific exercise.
- Often policy is portrayed as rational when it is simply pragmatic and incremental – policy makers, just as many people do in all walks of life, simply 'muddle through'.

Questions for consideration

1. Identify a criminal justice 'problem' in your area. Using the framework above, define and discuss the ideologies visible in any policy suggestions put forward by politicians.
2. What do you understand by the phrase 'non-decision making'? Why might this pose a problem for proponents of the rational model of policy making?
3. Critically explore Lukes' (2004) contention that there is a third face of power? In what ways do you think a population's desires could be shaped?
4. What potential is there for genuinely radical solutions to existing social, political and economic problems? How far would you go to resolve them from your own perspective? What might the consequences be?

5 Criminal justice policy makers and policy-making bodies in England and Wales

Introduction

How many times have you heard the phrase 'I wish *they'd* do something about crime'? or 'I wish *they'd* make sure that life sentences mean life sentences'? This chapter looks at just who 'they' are in relation to criminal justice policy in England and Wales. You should be aware that in this chapter we have included the names of some of the current key post-holders within the English and Welsh criminal justice system. However, these post-holders can and will change as the political and organisational landscape develops over time. As a result, if you are undertaking some work that requires naming officers or ministers of state you should check to see exactly who the current post-holder is instead of relying on the information contained in this chapter. One of the enduring features of academic writing is the endless qualification of statements and claims!

The purpose of this chapter is to introduce you to the often complex and ever-changing landscape of real world politics. Many of our local, regional, national and supra-national politicians are what can be called 'career politicians'; that is, they will have spent many years in political life and not 'worked' for many years. Indeed, there is a growing trend for politicians to have only ever worked within politics, starting life as aides or advisors and then moving onto electoral politics themselves as councillors, MPs or ministers. David Cameron, the current Prime Minister, has actually set a goal of recruiting more candidates with work experience beyond the world of politics. Nevertheless, research by the independent think-tank the New Local Government Network in 2009 showed that around 25 per cent of candidates selected by all political parties for the 2010 general election had never worked outside professional politics. The Conservatives were slightly less well represented, with a third of their candidates having served as aides or functionaries (McSmith, 2009). What is the problem? you may well ask. Why should it matter that politicians have worked only in their chosen field? After all, that is how other professionals in other areas obtain the skills and experience they need to perform well. We would not expect a consultant in the health service to spend half of their training in another field such as landscape gardening.

However, it has been argued that politics is not like other 'professions', that in order to 'practise' it effectively practitioners need life experience. Think about it. When we ask politicians to take responsibility for policy areas and for making and sanctioning decisions in areas that they may not have much prior experience in, we, at least in theory, create the potential for poor decision making. Equally, this chapter will show that supporting those politicians is a group of experienced civil servants who have often made life-time careers working, in our case, either in the Home Office or, more recently, in the Ministry of Justice. Given that the focus of this book is on the English and Welsh criminal justice system, the main part of the chapter will identify the key players and important ministerial and organisational structures within that system. However, in policy terms English and Welsh criminal justice policy is sometimes subject to decisions and directives which come from outside our borders, so before commencing with the more domestic information it is worth mentioning the impact that supra-national bodies such as the European Union (EU) or the United Nations (UN) can have on domestic criminal justice policy.

Supra-national bodies

Supra-national bodies and the supra-national policy they create can be defined as increasingly 'corporatist' (Falkner, 1998). In essence, it relates to laws and/or treaties that have no foundation in any domestic law but instead are created by multi-national bodies and then jointly recognised across a group of nation states. Richardson (1996) suggests that the optimum example of supra-national policy making is embodied by the EU, of which the UK is a member. As a result of that membership the UK is a signatory to a number of treaties and directives which can and do have an effect on the daily lives of its citizens or subjects.

One recent case in point is the adoption of the EU Convention on Human Rights 1950 directly into UK law in the form of the Human Rights Act (HRA) 1998, although Chakrabarti *et al.* (2010) argues that the Act was just as much a response to calls for a Bill of Rights. Nevertheless, it was informed by the Convention and has had a very significant impact on policy making in the criminal justice system (Cheney *et al.*, 2001), not least because the courts have used the legislation to frustrate the will of the executive (the government) on several occasions. Perhaps the most important arena for this confrontation has been the anti-terror measures passed in the wake of the attack on New York and other US targets in 2001. In the UK the architects of the HRA, New Labour, introduced a raft of anti-terror measures which ran counter to the principles of the law in general and specifically the HRA itself. Enshrined in law we have certain rights, which include:

- no detention without trial
- habeas corpus
- innocence until guilt is proven

- an open trial in court
- legal advice and representation
- just deserts in the allocation of punishment.

Of course these are 'principles' and there are areas of blurring and in some cases deviation (the punishment of sex offenders, for example, arguably goes beyond just deserts); nonetheless, they are held to be inviolable. However, with the passage of the anti-terror legislation from 2001 onwards, suspects were treated as guilty until proven innocent, they were held without trial (at one point the government sought a 90-day detention period), they were tried in closed proceedings, and some individuals were subject to extra-legal rendition. This reaction picks up on a point we made earlier in the book:

> Emergency legislation passed as a consequence of national catastrophe associated with terrorism has a predictable pattern. It involves an unseemly scramble between the Executive and legislature so that they are seen by the public and the media to be doing 'something'. A previously prepared emergency Bill is dusted down and hastily pushed through the legislature. Policy and law are thereby tightened, with scant recourse to reasoned chamber debate or recognition of standard procedures, in order to respond to the media and public outcry.
>
> (Thomas, 2002: 1196)

As a result of politicians wanting to be seen to be taking control, freedom came into conflict with the desire for security, or at least that was the way in which it was frequently presented. More recently, the government's pronouncements on accessing British citizens' emails and phone messages in the name of security have again brought into sharp focus the tensions between having to be seen to be 'doing something' in terms of the crimes associated with terrorism and erosion of, in this case, privacy and civil liberties.

In the face of this unravelling of legal and human rights, at times the judiciary stepped in and used the HRA to rebalance the scales. This was important in and of itself, but also because once 'extraordinary' legislation is accepted it tends to become 'normal' legislation (Hillyard, 1993, 2005) or, as we have said before, is passed off as a 'sensible' policy or decision. Arguments surrounding the practical value of counter-terror policies are important, as is the reality that vulnerable groups such as resident aliens and minority ethnic and religious groups are disproportionately adversely affected (Thomas, 2002; Landman, 2008). However, the larger issue revolves around justice, the maintenance of justice and the protection of civil liberties. The ongoing tensions created and the centrality of the HRA can be detected in this quote from Chakrabarti *et al.* (2010: 5):

> The HRA's political parents soon appeared impatient with its checks on executive power. After the Twin Towers' atrocity only eleven months

later, the Act was sometimes the sole practical protection against intern-
ment, evidence gathered through torture and breathtakingly broad police
powers passed in freedom's name.

The conflict between the judiciary and the executive arm of the state over the
rights of the individual became intense enough for the New Labour government
(who passed the Act) to seriously consider repealing it.

The UK is also a member of the United Nations. Here, the relationship between
the supra-national body and the member states is a little different from the relationship within the EU. The UN tends not to make 'laws' as such but instead
draws up treaties to which member states become signatories. For example, in the
field of illicit drugs the UN has produced a number of international treaties aimed
at firstly gaining an international agreement that certain substances should be
illegal and subsequently establishing some form of sanction for dealing in illicit
substances. However, these treaties tend to be statements of intent as opposed
to detailed policy documents. This is because in some instances the relationship
between these supra-national bodies and nation states revolves around a
principle called 'subsidiarity'. This means that the decision-making process is
devolved down to the lowest appropriate level. In practice this manifests as
major policy directions – the statements of intent – being taken at supra-
national level but the details – the stated aims – and the manner in which
policy is implemented – the plans of action – are devolved to national level.

Perhaps the best example of this, which most people are familiar with, is
the Netherlands' response to the criminalisation of cannabis by a succession
of UN treaties. Possession of cannabis is outlawed by international treaty and
as a result it must be seen as a criminal offence. However, whilst cannabis
possession is technically against the law in the Netherlands, in practice
the police will only prosecute people who are holding very large amounts and
are potentially supplying others (Cohen, 2003).

Thus, the EU and the UN can and are policy makers whose decisions will
affect Britain, but in most cases the implementation and final shape of the
policy will be decided at national level. However, the prohibitive framework
established by the UN and supported by major players such as the United
States actually threatens the basis for supra-national governance, as several
countries want greater room for liberalisation. According to Bewley-Taylor
(2003), in the future a collective formed of like-minded countries may seek
withdrawal from the treaties governing drug policies, which would significantly weaken the international regime represented by the UN. Cohen
(2003) agrees that change at the international level is unlikely, and maybe
even at the national level; the promise of change resides at the local level,
where countries like the Netherlands have led the way. In time, fortified by
unchallenged local revisions, a coalition of countries may find itself strong
enough to achieve drug reform and see it enshrined in a new treaty.

Thus, whilst in the main criminal justice policy in England and Wales is
made, administered and implemented via national and local government, it is

important that you are aware that certain aspects of domestic policy are influenced, and in some cases, particularly with EU legislation, directly affected, by policy which is made by bodies outside the national government. However, the fact remains that the vast majority of criminal justice policy is made by the UK government, and it is to the key players and underpinning structures of this policy system that we now direct our attention.

Just before we do this, it is important to note that, as we write, the government of the UK is in the hands of a coalition between the Conservative Party and the Liberal Democrats. As such this represents a new era in UK politics and poses some interesting questions regarding roles, responsibilities and dominant ideologies. For example, Nick Clegg is Deputy Prime Minister. We know that in theory at least he is an oft-consulted deputy and that there is at least consensus on some decisions, so we must assume that Mr Clegg is as instrumental in the making of, and thus as responsible for the outcomes of, government policy as Prime Minister David Cameron. Whether that is the case in reality remains to be seen but, as yet, it is too early to answer these questions authoritatively, so for the purposes of illustration we will assume that there is a shared approach to criminal justice policy amongst all Coalition members, or if that is stretching the scope of assumption too far, then at least we will assume that there is a willingness to compromise for the sake of making government possible.

The Prime Minister and the Cabinet

When thinking about the structure and organisation of just how criminal justice policy making in England and Wales works, we would argue that it is necessary to try to envisage the criminal justice policy-making structure as a pyramid. Notionally at the top of that pyramid is the Prime Minister, currently David Cameron, and, in principle at least, Nick Clegg as Deputy Prime Minister must sit just under that. This is not the place to provide detailed information on the role of the Prime Minister (for a very detailed account of the structure of the British state see Budge *et al.*, 1998: Ch. 8). However, in theory at least the British Prime Minister will have a huge impact on the shape, if not the exact detail, of criminal justice policy, largely for two reasons. First, crime has become one of the major political issues in contemporary Britain and it has proven to be a key electoral concern for the last two to three decades. If we reflect on the 2005 General Election, in the run up to it MORI – an independent market-research company – carried out a poll that showed crime was the most important political issue for 40 per cent of the people surveyed, compared to 36 per cent who named the health service and 26 per cent education. What is interesting about this is that crime was falling and was not a major factor in media coverage. Millie (2008: 109) carried out a review of the political literature and media coverage of that time, and argued that the reason crime was such an issue for the public was its politicisation by the two main parties. 'Law and order' rhetoric and policy resonate with the general public:

The public do regard crime as something that is important. However, the apparent lack of choice in criminal policy between the two main parties is a concern for the democratic process. Since the election, some of the rhetoric has changed; but Labour and the Conservatives have continued to follow *very* similar – and populist – paths.

It is in the Prime Minister's interest to ensure that criminal justice policy is working and that it fits with the political and ideological direction of the party. Of course if Millie is correct, then as opinion-formers this is almost certain to happen.

The second reason is that, as part of their remit and power, the Prime Minister appoints and fires ministers. As such, this changes the shape of departments such as the Home Office. As an example, when Labour held power former Home Secretary John Reid launched a major overhaul of the Home Office within days of being appointed. His approach was radical to the extent that a new ministry, the Ministry of Justice, was created. The Home Office retained responsibility for counter-terrorism, policing and asylum and immigration, while the Ministry of Justice took on the Department of Constitutional Affairs and the criminal justice functions of the Home Office, becoming the lead agency in terms of criminal justice policy (House of Commons Constitutional Affairs Committee, 2007). We will explore this division in more detail below.

Operating beneath the Prime Minister is the Cabinet. This is composed of senior figures from the government who represent all the major offices of state (for example the Chancellor of the Exchequer, the Home Secretary, the Foreign Secretary and so on). The Cabinet bears collective responsibility for the decisions of the executive, although under Tony Blair there were recurring questions about the inordinate degree of power that he sought as Prime Minister (Heffernan, 2003). For example, in her resignation letter former Development Secretary Clare Short said:

> The problem is the centralisation of power into the hands of the Prime Minister and an increasingly small number of advisers who make decisions in private without proper discussion ... There is no real collective responsibility because there is no collective; just diktats in favour of increasingly badly thought-through policy initiatives that come from on high. The consequences of that are serious. Expertise in our system lies in departments. Those who dictate from the centre do not have full access to that expertise and do not consult. That leads to bad policy.
>
> (Short, 2004)

There can be little doubt that Blair – just as Margaret Thatcher did before him – wanted to present his premiership as presidential in the style of American politics (Foley, 2000). But, as Heffernan (2003) suggests, this depends on the resources a Prime Minister has at his or her disposal and can only ever be temporary. Therefore, members of the Cabinet will have an indirect influence over criminal justice policy, as the whole Cabinet is informed of major policy developments and these are debated by Cabinet members. Yet whilst there is some collective responsibility over such decisions, it is fair to say that the relevant minister will take the lion's share of responsibility for the actions of their ministry.

At this stage it is worth noting the influence that the Chancellor of the Exchequer (currently George Osborne) can exert over criminal justice policy. The job of the Chancellor is to manage the country's financial affairs and as such to allocate funds and budgets to the various government departments and ministries. The amount each department gets fluctuates according to tax and borrowing revenues and the priorities placed upon the tasks that the ministries and departments carry out. Within the current political climate the Home Office's budget is, like that of most of the major offices of state, under scrutiny due to the Coalition's stated policy of reducing the budget deficit. That said, law and order and national security are clearly priorities for any government so, unlike for example the budget for welfare benefits (as we write disability benefits are under specific review), law and order is relatively well protected from the worst excesses of public spending cuts.

It is unlikely this will continue though, and already things are beginning to change even for previously favoured criminal justice agencies. Under Margaret Thatcher the police were supported for their role in breaking the unions and in managing the rise in crime that has been related to the deregulated economy the Conservatives set in train (Sullivan, 1998: 28). Little really changed under New Labour in terms of financial support, and in opposition David Cameron told Andrew Marr:

> Any cabinet minister, if I win the election, who comes to me and says: 'Here are my plans', and they involve front-line reductions, they'll be sent straight back to their department to go away and think again. After 13 years of Labour, there is a lot of wasteful spending, a lot of money that doesn't reach the front line.

Yet by 2015 front-line police officer numbers will be cut by 16,200, and Her Majesty's Inspectorate of Constabulary estimates that the eventual loss will be as high as 34,100. They further suggest that a 10 per cent fall in police numbers will see a 3 per cent increase in acquisitive crime (Eaton, 2011). This process has seemingly begun, with London reporting a rise in burglary in the capital of 19 per cent between May 2010 and the same time in 2011. Robberies rose 15 per cent in the same time period (http://www.londonnet.co.uk/news/2011/jun/london-crime-shoots-met-chief-concerned.html.). This indicates all too clearly that the favoured status of criminal justice agencies – even the police service – is subject to amendment given the right (or maybe the wrong) circumstances.

Below the Cabinet itself are a number of what are known as Cabinet committees. There are two types and, for our purposes in this book, we are concerned with the standing Cabinet committees. There are about 25 of these and, where possible, they are chaired by the minister with direct responsibility for the policy area. In criminal justice terms there are a number of standing committees, including those for anti-social behaviour and youth justice. Cabinet committees have two key purposes:

- to relieve the burden on the Cabinet by dealing with business that does not need to be discussed at full Cabinet
- to support the principle of collective responsibility by ensuring that even though a question may never reach the Cabinet itself, it will be fully considered. In this sense, Cabinet committee decisions have the same authority as Cabinet decisions.

More broadly, Cabinet committees provide a framework for collective consideration of, and decisions on, major policy issues and questions of significant public interest. They ensure that issues that are of interest to more than one department are properly discussed and that the views of all relevant ministers are considered. You may wish to consider how this level of consideration fits with the policy-making models discussed above, particularly the rational policy-making model.

The business of Cabinet and Cabinet committees is mainly made up of the following subjects:

- the co-ordination of particularly complex government business, such as the legislative programme, constitutional issues and public expenditure;
- questions which significantly engage the collective responsibility of the government because they raise major policy issues, or are of critical importance to the public;
- questions where there is an unresolved difference of opinion between departments.

Ministers and departments

The Home Office has a long history and has developed as a key government ministry over a period of time. However, it can be argued that it gradually became a 'catch-all' ministry that began to lose some of its sense of purpose. (This is clearly what John Reid, a former Home Secretary, had in mind when he stated that he felt the Home Office Immigration and Nationality Directorate was in need of fundamental reform and that the whole system was 'not fit for purpose' – Mulholland and Tempest (2006).) As a result its role and remit were not as clear cut as some of the other Ministries, whose role is reflected in their title. Over a period of two centuries the Home Office, and by extension the Home Secretary, had been assigned responsibility for a disparate and relatively large number of policy areas. As a result it became cumbersome and led ultimately to the break-up of responsibility and the creation of the Ministry of Justice in 2007, as stated above. This removal of some responsibility from the Home Office, coupled with the creation of a new ministry, has led to a substantial change in the manner in which central government manages and delivers criminal justice policy. It was formerly the case that the key minister in terms of criminal justice policy was the Home Secretary and the key department was the Home Office. On 9 May 2007 a new ministry, the Ministry of Justice, started work.

In effect, this split the Home Office into two separate ministries: one dealing with national security and the other with criminal justice and law. In practice the split meant that the Home Office lost control of criminal justice policy, including running the prisons and probation services, but importantly not policing. The Ministry of Justice acquired 50,000 former Home Office civil servants and the tasks of running the criminal justice system and reducing re-offending, including creating new criminal offences. It will also take in the responsibilities of the current Department of Constitutional Affairs. The new Home Office is responsible for policing, immigration and identity cards, as well as counter-terrorism, and will be more akin to a US-style department for homeland security. The division of labour and the responsibilities for each ministry are as follows:

1. Home Office

    - Office of Security and Counter-terrorism
    - crime and policing
    - anti-social behaviour
    - drugs policy
    - community safety
    - Serious Organised Crime Agency
    - Criminal Records Bureau
    - Borders and Immigration Agency
    - identity cards and passports

2. Ministry of Justice

    - National Offender Management Service, covering prisons and probation
    - criminal justice reform
    - criminal, civil and family law
    - youth justice
    - courts and tribunals, legal aid
    - supporting the judiciary
    - Privy Council
    - electoral reform
    - human rights
    - freedom of information
    - devolution

The current Home Secretary is Theresa May and the current Justice Minister is Ken Clarke (who has previously held the post of Home Secretary, with the distinction of being named by Civitas, the independent right-wing think-tank, as 'the worst Home Secretary ever'). Ken Clarke also has responsibility for the law and the courts and holds the title Lord Chancellor and so is the head of the judiciary. This is a break with the past and represents a new approach to governing criminal justice. The previous Lord Chancellor was Lord Falconer (who incidentally once shared a flat with Tony Blair, a former Labour Prime Minister – you might want to return to the chapter above that deals with elite groups in the policy-making process and reflect on this). Ministers in charge of government departments are usually in the Cabinet. They are known as 'Secretary of State' or may have a special title, as in the case of the Home Secretary.

Ministers of State are middle-ranking ministers. They normally have specific responsibilities and are sometimes given titles which reflect these functions, for example Minister for Police and Security. The most junior ministers are called Parliamentary Under-Secretaries of State or, where the senior minister is not a Secretary of State, simply Parliamentary Secretaries. They may be given responsibility, directly under the departmental minister, for specific aspects of the department's work. Ministerial responsibility refers both to the collective responsibility for government policy and actions which ministers share and to ministers' individual responsibility for the work of their own departments (adapted from www.directgov.uk, 2006).

We do not need to concern ourselves with the details of the work that each of the Ministries does at this stage; suffice it to say that generally speaking the Ministry of Justice runs the criminal justice system with the exception of the police (see the lists above for which organisation does what). The day-to-day roles of the Home Secretary and the Minister of Justice and the junior ministers in each department involve (Budge *et al.*, 1998: 231):

- administration of the department
- policy making, including meeting with counterparts in other departments
- politics; they are almost always serving MPs and have to attend Parliament and do constituency work
- public relations; they meet practitioners, the general public and deal with the media
- the European Union; they will work closely with European colleagues, especially on cross-border issues.

The MPs who are currently serving in the capacity of ministers and junior ministers in the Ministry of Justice (MoJ) are listed below alongside their jobs – or, in the correct jargon, their briefs.

- Lord Chancellor and Secretary of State for Justice – Kenneth Clarke
- Minister of State – The Rt. Hon. Lord McNally (civil liberties, freedom of information, data protection)
- Minister of State – The Rt. Hon. Nick Herbert MP (criminal justice strategy) works across the Home Office and MoJ
- Parliamentary Under-Secretary of State – Crispin Blunt MP (portfolio for prisons, probation, youth justice)

- Parliamentary Under-Secretary of State – Jonathan Djanogly MP (portfolio for legal aid, HM Courts Service, civil law, family law, coroners and burials)
- Only two Parliamentary Under-Secretaries of State are listed.
- The Permanent Secretary at the Ministry of Justice is Sir Suma Chakrabarti KCB.

(MoJ, 2012)

The ministers who make up the Home Office team are listed here:

- Home Secretary – Theresa May
- Minister of State – Nick Herbert MP (policing and criminal justice), works across Home Office and MoJ
- Minister of State – Lord Henley (crime prevention and anti-social behaviour reduction)
- Three Ministers of State – third one: Damian Green MP (immigration, asylum and border control)
- Parliamentary Under-Secretary – James Brokenshire MP (crime and security)
- Parliamentary Under-Secretary of State – Lynne Featherstone MP (criminal information)
- Only two Parliamentary Under-Secretaries of State.

(Home Office, 2012)

The civil servants

Before we examine the influence of what is arguably the most interesting group of national policy makers, it is important that you understand the distinction between 'Civil Servants' in the context of central government and 'civil servants' such as police officers and probation officers. The first group of people referred to here and the subject of the next section are permanent servants of the Crown, whereas the other group of people who are also known as civil servants are employed by an agency of the Crown, such as Devon and Cornwall Police. Whilst the name is the same, the importance and influence of the two types of civil servants vary enormously.

For our purposes, then, the Civil Servants working for the ministries are expected to perform their role in respect of four key features:

1. *Impartiality.* Because they are permanent, they are expected to serve equally well and neutrally whichever political party is in power.
2. *Anonymity.* They are anonymous when doing their work, and politicians cannot ask questions about their conduct or any advice they may give.
3. *Permanence.* Unlike in many other WLDs, top Civil Servants do not change when a government changes.
4. *Secrecy.* All Civil Servants sign the Official Secrets Act and any advice they give is correspondingly secret.

There are only about one thousand top Civil Servants in Britain and they are sometimes known as 'mandarins' because of the power and influence they wield. (For those of you who are interested, more information can be found at www.homeoffice.gov.uk/documents/org-chart-020806.pdf.) However, whilst they may be small in number, it is arguable that they are disproportionately large in influence, and it is to this level and degree of influence and power that the penultimate section of this chapter now turns.

Politicians, mandarins and the policy-making process

Most MPs, whilst having a university education, are generalists inasmuch as they do not have expert knowledge across all aspects of government policy. Even those 'professional' politicians who have worked as aides will have quite specific policy backgrounds in most cases. For back-bench MPs this may not matter, but for those charged with making policy it could be argued that their lack of knowledge is detrimental to their ability to make informed decisions on serious aspects of government work. For example, a previous Home Secretary, Alan Johnson, held the following parliamentary posts before becoming Home Secretary: Secretary of State for Health, Secretary of State for Education and Skills, Secretary of State at the Department of Trade and Industry, and junior minister at the Department of Work and Pensions. With so many different roles, how likely is it that an individual would have the requisite knowledge and experience to do them all equally well? *It may be just as legitimate to ask: 'how can a man with no prior experience of the criminal justice system possibly know enough to formulate the detailed, multi-faceted policies required to deal with the complexities of the "crime problem" at the same time as being responsible for dealing with all the other things an MP and minister is required to do?'*

The answer is clearly 'he cannot', and it is at this point that the power and influence of the mandarins come into play. Their longevity in post and their experience of formulating and evaluating policies in the past can and do influence their political masters. In theory, the mandarins are responsible for administration and the politicians are responsible for policy. However, in practice it is very difficult to see where and if there is a clear division between those two concepts. As a consequence, mandarins, in theory at least, possess a great deal of potential power and it has been suggested that it is they, not the elected politicians, who make the majority of policy. This has been the subject of a great deal of debate in the past and we need not enter into that degree of detail here. It is worth considering the quotes on page 240 of Budge *et al.* (1998) which provide a range of opinions on the power and influence of Civil Servants over policy decisions. The truth is that it is impossible to gauge the extent to which mandarins influence policy as the policy-making process involves a number of key players and is almost always influenced by outside agencies, political needs and external events. Hill (2005: 163–73) provides a detailed look at this debate. That said, at the very least you need to be aware that there is a group of unelected people, largely free from public scrutiny, who can and do wield enormous power and influence over criminal justice policy in England and Wales.

Conclusion

It should be clear that there are a number of key players involved in the policy-making process and that it is inconceivable that any policy is the work of just one person; rather, policy is a result of a number of discussions, meetings and planning events conducted over a period of time and often based on precedent and existing structures and agreements. As such, it may be that policy is more akin to the incremental pragmatism model simply because some of the main political players are reliant on their Civil Servant 'minders' for advice.

However, what we can say for sure is that policy is seldom static: it can and does change over time, and as such it is also important that you understand that the complexity of the policy process and the manner in which the key players can and do change over the course of a parliament may inhibit and indeed shape the types of policy which can be and are made.

Questions for consideration

1. What do you understand by the term 'supra-national'? Can you think of a criminal justice policy area where supra-national treaties and laws could be seen as essential?
2. Would it be a bad thing if British prime ministers became even more 'presidential'? Could it be that a good, strong leader would make better decisions?
3. Discuss the role of the 'mandarins'. In a liberal democracy should we know more about their roles and the advice they give? Is their background relevant to the work they do?

6 Policy implementation

Turning ideas into action

Introduction

In the previous two chapters we have looked at how policy is made and also identified some of the key people who are currently involved in making criminal justice policy in England and Wales. Both explicitly and implicitly we have focused on the role that politicians play in policy making. The inference is that policy making is the preserve of politicians, be they supra-national, national or local, suggesting that policy *doing* (implementation) is the preserve of officials, professionals and administrators. Whilst in reality this distinction is perhaps not as clear as we imply here, it is almost always the case that those that make policy and those that implement policy are different people. For example, the Justice Minister (currently Ken Clarke) is ostensibly responsible for *making* criminal justice policy but clearly he does not implement it. Thus, implementation of any policy that Ken Clarke makes becomes the responsibility of a number of criminal justice organisations and those people that work for them – the police, the courts, the prisons and so on.

At first glance this may seem simple but, as always, the more we examine the situation, the more complex it inevitably becomes. In certain contexts the design and implementation roles in policy work are actively blurred; for example, in the foreword to a practical guide to policy making Nigel Hamilton, Head of the Northern Ireland Civil Service, proposed that:

> One of the key messages which I hope this guide will help to send out is that policy development should not be seen as the preserve of a few specialists. Those involved at the 'front line' of service delivery, whether in schools, hospitals or social security offices, have a vital role in helping to gauge what is deliverable. They have a keen awareness of what really matters to the citizen. In order to develop policies which work in practice, the guide emphasises the importance of engaging those familiar with delivery issues, and service users themselves, early in the process.
>
> (Office of the First Minister and Deputy First Minister, 2003)

In all fairness this inclusive approach seems to be more popular in some policy contexts than others. This chapter guides you through some of the complexities integral to the making/implementation divide. Once this is done, we ask you to begin to think about how those that implement policy can and do affect the manner in which policy is delivered and thus how in turn that may affect the manner in which policy impacts on our day-to-day lives.

Policy making and policy implementation

This chapter continues a trend in policy studies literature by separating the formulation (making) of policy and the implementation (doing) of policy, but it is worth noting that the distinction between policy formulation and policy implementation is not so clear cut as may be suggested; for a full discussion see Hill (2005: 174–76). Essentially there are two arguments as to why we may wish both to study implementation separately and to make the distinction between formulation and implementation. These are (Stoker, 1998):

1. If people believe there is a distinction between policy making and policy doing, then it will affect their actions and we need to study what they do in order to look at the effects of such a distinction.
2. We need to be sceptical about this distinction and examine the power relations inherent within it. For example, it can be the case that powerful policy makers often use the distinction between policy making and policy doing to hide faults in the policy they design and thus shift the blame for a failed policy on to those charged with implementing it.

Therefore, we may need to be careful in making or believing claims for a clear cut distinction between the formulation of policy and its implementation. This is because the gap between those who make policy and those who deliver it may not be as wide as some would have us believe. It is arguably the case that the boundary between policy making and policy doing is blurred and that there is a great deal of overlap. For example, some front-line managers have the capacity to make low-level policy decisions, as in the case of police sergeants making decisions about which areas of a night-time economy to patrol. That can be seen as policy making, yet if the same police sergeants subsequently join the patrol that is clearly a practical shift towards policy doing.

It is fascinating that the civilianisation of policing, the extent of which is contested (Jones and Newburn, 2002; Mawby and Worthington, 2002), has created even greater complexities in divining where the boundary sits between policy making and implementation. For example, Paterson (2007: 315), in exploring the role of Electronic Monitoring (EM) operatives in the police service, suggests that:

> The policy implementation process is complicated by the position of EM officials as sub-contracted service providers operating in the commercial sector. This sub-contracted position generates a new politically contested arena in the bureaucratic process of putting governmental policy into

practice – an arena where commercial imperatives can come into conflict with both the managerial objectives of the Home Office and the day-to-day practical concerns of EM officers.

Not only has the changing nature of policing added a new dimension to accurately drawing lines around policy roles, but the incursion of private interests in the process has intensified this ongoing complexity.

However, despite this, for the purposes of this chapter we are going to look at policy implementation as something necessarily separate from policy making. So from here we move to explore the basic requirements that policy makers have to turn their ideas into action – to get their policy implemented. This is important because policy implementation cannot operate in an organisational vacuum; put simply, someone has to be able to do it within a framework that ensures consistency and fairness. The absence of this framework will mean that, however good the policy is in theory, the practical application may be flawed or, in the worst case scenario, non-existent.

The basic requirements of 'doing policy'

According to Colebatch (2002: 110–19), there are three key requirements to policy implementation and these will now be reviewed.

Authority

It should be obvious that in order for a policy to be implemented there needs to be someone with the authority to (a) make policy and (b) ensure that it is carried out. For example, it may be the case that a probation support worker wants to formulate a policy that enables those offenders on community sentences to complete their sentences in a more flexible manner. Yet, given that probation support workers are at the bottom of the probation hierarchy, they will not have the authority to formulate the policy (Aldridge, 1999). By the same token, those at the bottom of the hierarchy do not have the authority to ensure that policy is carried out.

One way we can think about authority in the policy process is as a chain, with authority emanating from the top (that is the government whether supra-national, national or local) and trickling down through organisations such as the police via a chain of command, for example Chief Constable, Assistant Chief Constables, Chief Inspectors, and so on all the way down to police constables on the beat. At each stage there will be different levels of authority and also different degrees of involvement with 'doing' policy. For example, it is highly unlikely that a Chief Constable will physically implement a public order policy in terms of actually being involved in arresting those who are drunk and disorderly. It does happen, as Craig Mackey, the Chief Constable of Cumbria Police Service, found when he went out on the beat with one of the community teams. It was supposed to be a fact-gathering exercise about responses to anti-social behaviour, but he was actually involved in two arrests and had to seize a stolen motor bike (McGowan, 2008). Of course, this is the exception rather than the rule, largely due to the fact that Mr Mackey is not primarily employed as a beat officer.

Expertise

Implicit in any policy formulation and implementation is the presence of expertise. It should be self-evident that in order to 'do' policy those charged with implementing it should have the required level of expertise to implement the policy effectively, safely, according to any regulations and so on. Yet that level of expertise need not always be practical. For example, in terms of criminal justice, governments and local authorities often consult criminologists for their expertise in research and theory and ask them to feed into the formulation process despite – in the majority of cases – those academics having little or no practical experience in the delivery of policy. This has become even more important in recent times, with New Labour emphasising the centrality of evidence-based practice (Wells, 2004), a trend that has continued under the Conservative-led Coalition.

One of the interesting features of this discussion is the appropriate role for academic and research experts as participants in the policy process. It is widely accepted that the intellectual field of criminology is more than simply a way of understanding 'crime', criminals and criminal justice processes; it is also about informing and improving policy. How far it is successful in this is a point of contention:

> the bullishness and even boastfulness that accompanies the apparent vitality as an academic discipline ... is at odds with criminology's more limited success in shaping the public discussion of 'its' issues and its faltering influence on public policy and decision making.
>
> (Garland and Sparks, 2000: 191)

The issue of influence is vital, but so too is the orientation that criminological researchers adopt or are allowed to adopt in the actual construction of policy. Some clearly feel that criminological researchers ought to be more fully involved and that, in order for evidence-based policy to become a reality, they *have* to be more involved and at every stage (Duke, 2001). Others suggest that criminology is something of an art form rather than an exact science and that the research it produces will only ever have a very limited impact in real terms (Leavitt, 1999), while some believe that researchers ought to remain outside policy in order to avoid being co-opted and their critical voice effectively suppressed (Platt, 1984). Often these viewpoints are driven by the 'school' of criminology an individual hails from, which in turn reflects their ideological standpoint (we refer you back to the discussion on ideology in chapter 3).

At the same time as expertise drawn from within research and other fields is significant, there is also a need for practical expertise in the shape of those charged to deliver and implement the policy – in short, if we formulate a policy which is dependent on 'the police', then we need to make sure that we have the expertise available within 'the police' to implement the changes. For example, we may wish to implement a new policy that arms all those police officers with a patrol function. However, in order to make that policy work most effectively, it would require all police officers with the possibility of undertaking a patrol function to have weapons training. Thus, in the short to medium term implementing the policy would be flawed due to a lack of expertise in terms of using weapons within the police service. Clearly, this lack of expertise could be rectified in the longer term. However, if we were to introduce a completely new policy, it may be the case that finding and training people with the necessary knowledge and skills will take a very long time to organise and major investment in order to make it reality.

A good example of the difficulties involved in this can be found in the movement of careers support for ex-offenders away from the prison and probation services towards the Employment Service (ES). The rationale for the move was clear, that the ES had the expertise and experience to best assist ex-offenders into employment – a critical role considering the emphasis placed on paid employment as a means of preventing/ending social exclusion, perhaps even providing the basis of modern citizenship for people of working age. Research indicated that the ES staff were often unwilling to help ex-offenders, and even where they were keen to support this new client group, their understanding of their experiences and needs was all too often limited. The problems with this policy innovation were twofold. First, while the existing provision was patchy and inconsistent, there were examples of good practice that were simply brushed aside. Second, the investment and time required to produce an effective, coherent and comprehensive system were felt to be more than would actually be forthcoming (Metcalf *et al.*, 2001).

Order

Once policy makers have both the authority to ensure that policy will be implemented in the required manner and the necessary expertise in place, they then need either an existing organisational framework within which to deliver policy or the ability to create/merge existing arrangements to create a new delivery framework. This could have been explored in the case of employment support for ex-offenders set out above, but the preference was to replace the old framework with something which made intuitive sense but which was arguably neither adequately planned and resourced nor well implemented. Equally, in terms of joint working (which we will look at in depth in another chapter), policy makers need to ensure that there is agreement and common ground across a host of areas. For example, in the case of child abuse, is there agreement about what constitutes abuse? Do the processes correspond across institutional boundaries? Are the IT systems compatible? Is there mutual respect between the police, the courts and social services? And so on. A failure to have this order in place runs the risk of undermining the policy during the implementation phase.

Hopefully, you will be able to see that these three factors act to both enhance and constrain the ability of policy makers to make and implement policy, at least in the short to medium term, and have a clear resonance with the previous two chapters in respect of what can and cannot be done in terms of formulating and implementing new policy. Having explored what is needed in order to begin to implement a policy, we now move on to pay more attention to the practicalities of making policy 'work'.

Implementing policy – making it work 'on the ground'

Planning is something that we do most of the time, and without some form of planning the popular notion of human activity is that it is directionless, maybe even pointless. Certainly in literature this reality has been recognised:

> 'Would you tell me which way I ought to go from here?' asked Alice. 'That depends a good deal on where you want to get,' said the Cat. 'I really don't care where,' replied Alice. 'Then it doesn't much matter which way you go,' said the Cat.
>
> (Lewis Carroll, *Alice's Adventures in Wonderland* (1865))

The transition from an idea – the formulation of a policy in response to a defined social problem often based on ideologically informed normative values – to a working policy that people can 'do' is a potentially dangerous time for policy makers, especially if they are elected politicians. This is because once the policy has left the abstract world of ideas, it becomes part of an increasingly messy 'real world' system which contains unknowable and uncontrollable events, ambiguities, interpretation gaps and such like. As a result the politicians begin to lose control. You know this happens from examples drawn from your own life. How many times have you planned a journey and left home in plenty of time only to end up being late because of an unexpected occurrence such as a breakdown, traffic jam or accident? It is the same principle with policy makers – once the policy is exposed to the real world, all sorts of unknowable and uncontrollable events can overtake and undermine the policy.

During a speech delivered at the headquarters of NATO (North Atlantic Treaty Organisation) in Brussels about the 'War on Terrorism' prosecuted by the Bush administration in the wake of the events of 11 September 2001, US Secretary of Defense Donald Rumsfeld made the following statement about formulating relevant policy:

> Now what is the message there? The message is that there are no 'knowns'. There are things we know that we know. There are known unknowns.

That is to say there are things that we now know we don't know. But there are also unknown unknowns. There are things we don't know we don't know. So when we do the best we can and we pull all this information together, and we then say well that's basically what we see as the situation, that is really only the known knowns and the known unknowns. And each year, we discover a few more of those unknown unknowns.

(http://www.nato.int/docu/speech/2002/s020606g.htm)

There was a great deal of amusement about the seeming lack of clarity in this statement at the time in different quarters of the media, politics and academia, which Rumsfeld himself acknowledged: 'It sounds like a riddle. It isn't a riddle. It is a very serious, important matter' (ibid.). Where the quote makes sense, and is thus worth repeating and examining here, is in its emphasis on the continual lack of information policy makers have to work with, something that would not surprise economic liberals, as this has always been at the root of their misgivings about political activity. This is why the market place is perceived to be more effective because it works according to laws of supply and demand that direct an invisible hand in order to maximise welfare outcomes, whereas state actors cannot replicate this because they only have informational fragments to work with (Hayek, 1944; Friedman, 1962).

Our objective, however, is to underline the difficulties that attend policy making by those working on behalf of the state. Dorey (2005: Ch. 7) lists eight prerequisites for the perfect implementation of policy which are central to our understanding of what can and does cause policy to falter and sometimes fail. What follows is an adaptation of Dorey's framework for our own purposes.

1. External agencies or events do not pose major constraints

Clearly, this cannot ever happen in the real world – there are always constraints and often they are completely unexpected. For example, who could have predicted that on 10 September 2001 the British police would be required to dramatically increase their anti-terrorist capacities? Or similarly, how could it be known that in the summer of 2011 they would be required to respond to a series of urban riots across several English cities and towns? Equally, the recent global financial crisis has led to swingeing cuts in public policy which many policy makers did not foresee yet has significantly impacted on their ability to construct and implement policy. It is of course also important to recognise, particularly in this latter example, the role that ideology plays in interpreting the nature of events as external constraints.

2. Dependency relationships are minimal

In an ideal world those charged with implementing a policy would be able to work in isolation from any other agency. Again, this does not reflect the real world. Indeed, since the early 1980s and increasingly since the election of

New Labour in 1997, there has been a growth in 'joined-up working' which requires the input of several agencies in the implementation of government policy. Far from being a problematic shift in organisational policy and practice, inter-agency work was conceived as the ideal means of closing some of the information gaps identified above, of seeing the problems individuals have as complex and spanning the remits of different agencies, and of tackling what New Labour referred to as 'social exclusion'.

Of course, this idealistic standpoint did not take into account the reality of 'joined-up' working:

> This conception of interagency working rests upon 'non-conflictual' models of collaboration, in which the horizontal tensions that exist between different agencies and the vertical tensions that exist across different hierarchical levels are largely denied and consensus or 'shared' professional values or cultures are enshrined as the basis for interagency working. Moreover, many of the studies which do problematise interagency working adopt a narrowly systemic approach, focusing upon managerial or technological 'barriers' to effective interagency collaboration.
>
> (Warmington *et al.*, 2004: 1–2)

Operating in isolation might be the best possible scenario from the perspective of individual agencies and their representatives, but this is not an option in the modern policy-making and policy-doing world. In fact, joined-up working is the new reality, with all the problems and possibilities this entails. Moreover, this will only intensify with the Big Society project of the Coalition government elected in 2010, as volunteers and third-sector organisations are tasked with filling the gaps left by a state in retreat (Smith, 2010).

3. There are a minimal number of decision points

It is often the case that those charged with implementing a policy (sometimes referred to as 'street level bureaucrats') have to make decisions as to how to interpret the policy. This is because it is practically impossible for the policy makers to construct a policy that covers every possible scenario that the street level bureaucrats will encounter. Consider the difference between making a policy about how to serve a customer with fast food and making a policy about patrolling a neighbourhood with diverse teams on the beat. In the former case, it is possible to prepare a stock set of questions that uncovers the customer's requirements and so ensure that the order is prepared and served correctly. Given the relatively small menu most fast food outlets provide, there is very little need for the server to display any level of discretion or autonomy. However, compare that with the complexities and ever-changing nature of a police officer and support professionals patrolling a beat. In this case, the officer or support professional will experience routine encounters that could be 'scripted' for, but equally they will be placed in situations that require a high degree of autonomy and discretion. Making a 'one-size-fits-all' policy for the latter is beyond the realms of possibility.

As a result, there is ample scope for street level bureaucrats to interpret and thus subvert, either on purpose or accidentally, the goals of the original policy makers. The more decision points there are, the more likely it is that the original aims and goals of the policy makers will be subverted.

Stop and think for a moment: it is likely that we can probably all recount examples in which we shift between the roles of policy maker and policy 'doer', where in the process of implementing policy we actually change or revise it. For example, on a bus journey recently one of the authors entered into a conversation with a woman about her new job. She had taken a Christmas retail job working for one of the big high-street department stores. Her role was to work on the tills, stock the shelves and help with any general enquiries from customers. As part of her induction, she was informed that it was the store's policy to offer *every* customer a loyalty card whilst serving on the till, and we could say without fear of contradiction that in this context she was merely a policy 'doer' and at a very junior level. However, within days she had decided that she would only offer loyalty cards to those she thought could afford to have one – thus she screened out certain older people and those who looked (from their dress, manner and appearance) as if they might be struggling financially. For the moment forget the stereotyping involved in her personal decision making; this informal policy shows the shift that frequently occurs between policy roles, and the major problems policy makers face in ensuring that their original plans are carried out.

4. Resources are adequate

You should not think of resources as only money – resources also relate to staff, time and knowledge. Implementing a policy without adequate resources becomes difficult. For example, you will have seen or heard the phrase 'prison crisis', earlier in this book if nowhere else, which relates to the problems that are created by overcrowded prisons. At the time of writing the statistics produced by the Ministry of Justice for the week beginning 10 February 2012 show that the current prison population stands at 88,388, while the useable capacity is 89,256. This means that the prison system is 868 places off reaching its complete capacity (http://www.justice.gov.uk/publications/statistics-and-data/prisons-and-probation/prison-population-figures/index.htm). The prediction is that the number will grow by at least 1,000 over 2012 as those involved in the 2011 riots are convicted.

One policy which would ease this situation is to build more prisons. This has been a key response by successive governments since the pronouncement by the then Home Secretary, Michael Howard, in 1993 that 'prison works' (Cavadino and Dignan, 2007). Indeed, the prison growth predicted for 2012 will partly be alleviated by the opening of two new prison establishments: HMP Thameside in southeast London with a capacity of 900 and HMP

Featherstone 2 with 1,600 places (BBC News, 2011a). However, new buildings take time to design, get through the planning process and finally construct. Another way to ease the prison crisis would be to increase the numbers of prison officers, but again this is a resource-heavy policy and would depend on having an adequate infrastructure in the first place. Given that we are in a period of retrenchment of public spending, it is unlikely that either option will happen in the current political cycle.

It might be that we need to look elsewhere for a resolution to the crisis in the penal system. Stella (2001: 58) suggests, for example, that 'social policy is the best criminal policy'. In similar vein, Cavadino and Dignan (2007) offer what they call a 'radical pluralist' alternative which entails not only considering different penal policies but also exploring the causes of crime, which might lead us to feel less punitive and seek to prevent crimes from happening in the first place. Of course, this would also require a large investment of resources, firstly in identifying where and how crime might be prevented and secondly in operationalising consistent policy options. Whatever we do, or as we mentioned earlier whatever 'they' do, there will be resource implications and particularly in this current age of austerity (assuming that things really are as they are represented politically, then this is going to be an issue for many years to come).

5. Policy is based on a valid theory of cause and effect

All policy is based on the assumption that there is a cause and effect. To return to the example used in a previous chapter, anti-social behaviour is caused by a lack of facilities and therefore the solution (policy) is to improve leisure facilities for young people. However, as we have seen above, in most aspects of criminal justice policy there are generally a number of alternative 'causes'. If the policy makers and their experts have got the 'cause' wrong, then the policy is doomed to fail. Some commentators, as we have already mentioned, actually suggest that policy makers deliberately 'misidentify' causes, which obviously means that, unless by some cosmic coincidence they touch unexpectedly on the true cause (assuming there is one), the policy alternatives will fail (Edelman, 2001). When this occurs, according to Edelman, the next step is to increase the intensity with which the policy is enforced, and so a cycle of monumental failure is inevitably set in train.

Even if we dispute the case presented by Edelman, it is still apparent that establishing the causes of crime presents a serious problem for criminal justice policy makers as there is major disagreement as to what the relevant causes of crime are, and at various times in the political cycle different interpretations take precedence. To complicate things further, different views are manifest even within the same party, with quite spectacular changes in policy. As Conservative Home Secretary responsible for the passage of the Criminal Justice Act (CJA) 1991, Douglas Hurd questioned the value of imprisonment as a means of tackling most criminal behaviour. Indeed he described it as 'an expensive way to make bad people worse' (Cavadino and Dignan, 2007). This suggested that most crime was opportunistic not premeditated, and so using prison sentences as a form of deterrence was neither practically effective nor cost effective. The CJA 1991 was consequently (mostly) informed by a retributive theory of punishment where individuals receive their 'just deserts'. Within two years – as set out briefly above – Michael Howard, who had taken on the role of Home Secretary, boldly stated that 'prison works'. This view stemmed from what we call reductivism, the desire to use punishment as a means of reducing crime, based on the supposition that criminals are rational actors who calculate the odds of being caught and who will therefore be less inclined to break the law when faced with harsh punishments (the evidence does not appear to bear this view out on the whole, as the certainty of detection appears to be more influential than the severity of the eventual sanctions; ibid.). So, not only did the main understanding of the causes of crime shift, but also the way in which crime should be dealt with changed course. When you consider that both were Conservatives, the huge uncertainty that surrounds important social and political questions is confirmed.

6. *The objectives are clear, coherent and consistent*

This relates to the overall aim or goal of the policy – in short, what exactly are particular policies trying to achieve? The more complex the policy, the less coherent and consistent it will by definition become. Again, clarity and consistency may be achievable when only one organisation is involved, but consider the effects when multiple agencies are charged with implementing a policy. With different histories, orientations, goals and targets and with specific budgets to protect, the objectives of policy as originally set out can be obscured at best and completely lost at worst (Pollitt, 2003). Equally, as in the case of problematic drug users, the policy may call for 'recovery' but implementing this to allow a full recovery will include some or all of the following: the police, the health sector, the courts, probation services, housing, social services, Jobcentre Plus. Whilst each of those agencies will have a part to play, there may well be disagreement as to what the agency-specific objectives are, how to achieve them and how to measure them.

7. *The objectives are fully understood and/or accepted by street level bureaucrats*

It is vitally important for those who formulate policy that their goals and aims in formulating the policy are fully understood; otherwise the policy is likely to fail. A major problem in trying to create a coherent framework across a vast edifice such as the criminal justice system of the UK is its complexity and sheer size. Brownlee (1998), early in the New Labour period, argued that there was an irreconcilable contradiction at the heart of the government's criminal justice programme. They emphasised the need for tough 'law and order' measures, manifesting a popular punitiveness that would increase prison numbers and in turn public expenditure. Aside from the capital required to build new prisons, keeping people maintained within them, according to the Prison Reform Trust, requires around £170,000 for each new place to be built and resourced, and £41,000 per annum per prisoner (BBC News, 2010). Unfortunately, another priority was to improve economic and efficiency outcomes through tighter managerial control and clearly these two objectives were in direct conflict. Despite support from professionals in the beginning, there was confusion – and some disillusionment – as the programme unfolded (McLaughlin and Muncie, 2000).

Just as importantly, if the rationale for the measures is not accepted by those that implement the policy, then it is just as often doomed to fail. In 1980 Lipsky argued in a ground-breaking study – which we have alluded to already and will consider in more detail below – that those responsible for implementing policy can have a serious impact on policy outcomes. Indeed they can even totally alter a policy by virtue of the discretion they exercise in carrying out their duties; of course, the degree of discretion will vary according to the role, with police officers on the beat potentially having more freedom to act than judges in a courtroom. At times those responsible for implementing policies can actually kill the germ of an idea from the outset. In the wake of the riots that shook several English cities during the summer of 2011, Prime Minister David Cameron looked to the United States for experience and ideas about how policing could be more effectively tailored to prevent their recurrence. Former US Police Chief William Bratton was initially consulted about dealing with street gangs due to his record of tackling gangs in his native New York; gangs were believed by the Conservatives to have been central to the occurrence of the riots. However, Hugh Orde, President of the Association of Chief Police Officers, dismissed the idea in the strongest of terms:

> I am not sure I want to learn about gangs from an area of America that has 400 of them … It seems to me, if you've got 400 gangs, then you're not being very effective. If you look at the style of policing in the States, and their levels of violence, they are so fundamentally different from here.
> (http://www.indianexpress.com/news/
> police-hit-out-at-camerons-hiring-of-us-cri/831881/)

Little was said about involving Mr Bratton after this, suggesting that not only can policies falter in the face of resistance by street level bureaucrats (albeit high level bureaucrats), but at times budding policy propositions can actually be totally abandoned.

8. Those at whom a policy is targeted respond in the expected manner

Generally speaking, the British are thought to be a compliant national community and we are seen by many (both from without and within) to respond to policies in the way the policy makers wish. However, from time to time laws are passed which are patently either wrong or unenforceable. For example, using a mobile phone whilst driving is considered a serious offence, and it is worth setting this out in some detail:

It is illegal to drive a vehicle or ride a motorcycle while using a hand-held mobile phone. This also applies to any similar device (that must be held at some point) to:

- send or receive spoken or written messages or still or moving images
- access the internet.

These devices include smartphones or Personal Digital Assistants (PDAs).

While driving, you must not use your hand-held mobile phone, smartphone or PDA:

- to make or receive calls
- to send or receive picture and text messages
- to access the internet
- when you're stopped at traffic lights
- when you're queuing in traffic.

It's also illegal to use a hand-held phone when supervising a learner driver or rider.

If you're an employer, you can be prosecuted if you ask your employees to make or receive calls while driving.

(http://www.direct.gov.uk/en/TravelAndTransport/
Roadsafetyadvice/DG_188761)

As befits such a serious offence, the penalties are quite harsh, a £60 fine and three points on the driving licence. However, it can mean a court case and a fine of up to £1,000, and for professional drivers the penalties are more severe.

For those who believe that people are rational calculators and likely to be deterred by severe sanctions (known theoretically as reductivists), this level of punishment should be sufficient to prevent driving and using the phone. Yet the annual report produced by the Royal Automobile Club (RAC) for 2011 showed that in the preceding 12 months:

- 27% of drivers admitted using a phone which was not hands-free
- 15% while stopped at traffic lights
- 37% of drivers 17–24 years of age admit these offences
- 38% of those aged between 25–44 admit these offences.

(RAC, 2011: 52)

Over 50 per cent of drivers surveyed expressed concern about the use of phones while others are driving. The report also indicates that the problem of driver distraction will probably become even more prevalent with the smart-phones now available, where drivers can readily access their email accounts and use the internet (ibid.).

There is a wealth of research indicating the dangers attached to driving while using a phone, stretching back to 1991 (Brookhuis *et al.*, 1991; Haigney *et al.*, 2000; Treffner and Barrett, 2004). Furthermore, as the RAC report shows, over half of the surveyed drivers were concerned about it, and the penalties are relatively harsh, as we have shown, and yet people continue to take the risk (and impose it on others). Why this should be so is an important question but not for our purposes. The truth is that the refusal to comply with the law and the potential for this to increase illustrate the weakness of the policy framework, though not the certainty of its ultimate failure, of course.

Equally, it is possible to argue that the downgrading of cannabis was a direct response to the extent of cannabis use in Britain, and the policy of prosecuting the personal use of the drug ran contrary to people's behaviour (Monaghan, 2008). The relationship between policy making and the behaviour of those targeted is extraordinarily complicated. Nevertheless, faced with a refusal to comply, any policy will be strained, sometimes to breaking point.

The implementation gap

It is arguable that fully achieving those eight points will be impossible, and as a result policies almost always suffer from what is known as 'the implementation gap' we have covered at length above. Some of this revolves around the fact that governments can neither know nor control events, a situation that has become worse and will continue to worsen the more 'globalised' the world becomes. Put simply, unexpected events happen which can cause existing policy to become outdated or redundant, and unexpected events can also lead to a shift in resources or the requirement of new forms of expertise, all of which undermines the plans of the policy makers; all of these, and additionally often unknowable or unforeseen factors, can quite literally occur overnight.

Whilst the impact of external factors on policy implementation is important and you need to recognise the effects these unknowable factors have on the implementation of policy, our main concern here is to explore the impact of the so-called 'street level bureaucrats' on the shape and delivery of policy. To a large extent the reason for the existence of a gap between the way the policy is formulated and the manner in which it is delivered lies with those who are charged with 'doing policy'. For the sake of consistency we will use the term 'street level bureaucrats' as a catch-all descriptive term. However, just to clarify, within criminal justice policy these will include, amongst others:

- judges
- magistrates
- Crown Prosecution workers
- police officers
- prison officers
- probation officers
- PCSOs

- drug workers
- hostel workers
- contractors employed to provide support and assistance to offenders (for example education, employment and training).

Writers such as Lipsky (1980) suggest that if you think about the roles that the professionals we have identified in the list above perform, you will see that in many criminal justice organisations street level bureaucrats have large degrees of autonomy and discretion. This enables them to interpret policy to fit their own goals and ideologies and/or their organisation's goals and ideologies, or more often than not a combination of both. As a result, policy on the ground can often look different from the manner in which it was envisaged during the planning stage. If Lipsky's contention is true, it means that those that deliver policy have as much influence on the manner in which the policy is delivered and received by its target group as those that make policy. We invite you to reflect on the anecdote set out earlier about the woman deciding who should be offered a store card and who should not be 'pressured', but more than this it may be useful to reflect on your own experience. In your own work, in playing for a sports team, or any other activity, consider the times that you have ignored or reshaped a policy decision.

Indeed, some authors go further and suggest that street level bureaucrats are *the* policy makers. Lipsky encapsulates this by claiming that 'the decisions of the street level bureaucrats ... effectively become the public policies they carry out' (Lipsky, 1980: xii).

What Lipsky is saying is that street level workers adapt and interpret policies in a way which enables them to cope with the stresses and strains of working with the public and which allows them to get through their working day with the minimum of fuss and stress. Lipsky justifies this argument by pointing out that dealing with the public is uncertain and will always be characterised by the need to react in a way that cannot possibly be planned by policy formulators, a point we made above in our two examples. Lipsky addresses this very succinctly:

> The essence of street level bureaucracies is that they require people to make decisions about other people. Street level bureaucrats have discretion because the nature of service provision calls for human judgement that cannot be programmed and machines cannot substitute.
>
> (Lipsky, 1980: 161)

Much of the discretion held by street level bureaucrats revolves around the difference between formal and informal operating procedures and the impact these have on implementing policy. Essentially, formal operating procedures are the rules and regulations set out by policy makers and organisations concerning the manner in which work will be conducted and the processes and procedures that need to be followed. Informal operating procedures relate to the manner in which work is actually performed and as a result is bound up in the discretion held by, in our case, criminal justice workers. Another way to look at it is as the 'that's-the-way-we-do-things-here' approach. Following on from that, the manner in which the street level bureaucrat interprets policy and employs discretion will have a direct and substantial effect on the manner in which the policy is experienced by those it is aimed at.

For example, the police have a duty to uphold the Queen's peace and to maintain law and order. Implicit within that is the formal requirement to stop, question and apprehend all those that the police witness breaking the law. At various times the government promotes policies which target this duty at specific types of behaviour. Recently, the government has been concerned with the actions of young people in relation to 'anti-social behaviour' and have encouraged the police to clamp down on anti-social behaviour wherever and whenever they see it.

Clearly that does not, and could not, happen as instructed, as very few police patrols, either in the car or on foot, would ever get more than a few hundred metres from the station before the police officers witnessed something which could be construed as anti-social behaviour. In the real world, police officers use discretion (often influenced by stereotyping and the impact of workplace culture) to decide when to stop, who to stop and how to react. As a result, the clamp down on anti-social behaviour is felt differently at different times and by different sections of society. Whilst in a way this level of discretion can be seen to be understandable and based on practical necessities, it needs to be qualified as the discretion enjoyed by police officers is seen as the foundation of discrimination against disadvantaged communities (Reiner, 1995; Waddington, 1999; Holdaway and O'Neill, 2006).

Arguably this level of discretion by street level bureaucrats is necessary as it allows those charged with implementing policy enough leeway to be able to implement policy in a way that reflects the multitude of social situations to which it may apply because, as we noted above, policy makers often cannot cover all eventualities and scenarios that street level criminal justice workers may face in the undertaking of their day-to-day duties. If you were given the task of formulating a policy relating to anti-social behaviour, could you provide a rule-based policy that distinguished between youthful exuberance and anti-social behaviour and feel sure that your rule-bound policy covered every conceivable situation? We would suggest that you could not and that ultimately you would become as reliant on the interpretation and autonomy of those charged with the delivery of policy as successive governments have become.

The problem that policy formulators have is that they have very little control over the way in which policy is interpreted and therefore are at least partially reliant on street level bureaucrats for the 'success' or 'failure' of their policy. Battle has arguably been joined most forcefully between policy makers and policy doers as criminal justice professionals since the 1980s, though for a while the police were protected and favoured (see McLaughlin, 1993), and this battle looks set to continue, and indeed in an age of austerity to intensify, for some time to come.

Conclusion

This chapter has provided a very brief look at the problems associated with implementing policy. It is important that you recognise the following points:

- Policy implementation and policy formulation are often different sides of the same coin.
- We can identify a number of prerequisites for the perfect implementation of policy.
- In the real world these prerequisites are unobtainable.
- Street level bureaucrats and the impact of what we can call informal operating procedures have a large influence on the manner in which policy is delivered and felt.
- The implementation gap is a real concern to policy makers as it has the potential to undermine their political and ideological policy goals.

Questions for consideration

1. Identify a recent criminal justice-based policy. Can you identify the point where 'policy making' becomes 'policy doing'? Should we be concerned about the distinction between policy making and policy implementation?
2. Above we noted that, in order for a policy to 'work', one of the requirements is for the target group to respond in the appropriate manner. This is clearly not the case in all manner of criminal justice policy. In those policy cases where there is mass law breaking does this mean the policy is flawed?
3. What do you understand by the term 'street level bureaucrats'? In your opinion, how important are they in the policy process?
4. When and how have you acted to thwart the aims of a formal policy? Did you think about the process behind the policy? Did your actions produce a better outcome? If so, who for?

7 Joint working

Introduction

As we have seen in the previous chapter, making policy 'work' can be fraught with difficulties, not least because of the actions of the people charged with delivering policy. However, increasingly over the past twenty years agencies which implement criminal justice policy have been asked to work in conjunction with other agencies from both within and outside the criminal justice system. Whilst there is plenty of evidence to suggest that this has enhanced service delivery in many cases, there is equally little doubt that it has made policy implementation that bit more complex.

This chapter is aimed at introducing you to the basic concepts and practices of working together. For our purposes, where agencies come together to address a social problem and deliver a set of services this will be referred to as 'joint working'. Having said that, should you undertake further reading in this area (which you almost certainly should do, especially in the fields of crime prevention, child protection and drug misuse) you will also see this particular approach to policy implementation called 'multi-agency working', 'inter-agency working', 'partnership', 'joined-up working', 'inter-agency coordination'. Lloyd *et al.* (2001: 3) provide the following framework for distinguishing between the different labels you will inevitably encounter:

- Interagency working – this refers to those instances where more than one agency work together in a planned and structured way. This can operate at the operational (implementation) or at the more strategic (decision-making) level.
- Joint working – when professionals work across agency or institutional boundaries on a joint project; for example, the police might work with teachers, social workers and other professionals to co-ordinate a project in schools on risk awareness.
- Multi-agency working – here more than one agency engages with an individual, family or project but not necessarily together.

McInnes (2007) on behalf of Barnardo's adds in the notion of 'partnerships' by taking into account work that is done beyond the borders of professionals and their employing agencies and involves contributions from the community and third-sector partners. This further reflects the growing policy complexities created by a mixed economy approach, and it appears that policies supporting current exhortations towards a 'big society' will further increase the number of agencies involved in delivering criminal justice policy. As a result, it is increasingly the case that we need to examine individual projects in order to determine and correctly label the specific nature of the joint working which is taking place.

As Lloyd *et al.* (2001) suggest, there is a tendency to use the terms multi-agency and interagency interchangeably but this would, using their model, be most inappropriate as they exist at different ends of the spectrum – from least (multi-agency) to most (interagency) collaboration. Whilst we do acknowledge these differences in terminology, the essence of the labels remains the same: more than one agency is working in a policy area to deliver services to the same client group. What we are trying to capture here is the work agencies do jointly, and though we are incorporating their categories of interagency and joint working, we will occasionally employ different terms predominantly to remain faithful to the published work of authors in the field.

This chapter examines the history and development of joint working. From there it moves on to look at the mechanics and the problems of joint working. It is worth noting that this is a huge area which could feasibly be a course on its own. As such, it has generated much research and theory and a whole body of literature. This chapter will only provide you with a basic overview of joint working (for a fuller account see Barton, 2002: chapter 2; Douglas, 2008), in order that you begin to understand this essential aspect of policy implementation.

A brief rationale for joint working

If we were to look back at academic and practice-based texts dealing with public and social policy published in the 1960s and 1970s, we would find little or no reference to agencies working together to address social problems (with the possible exception of those working within the area of child protection and even then these would be very loose arrangements). This is because, historically, British public administration has been organised around a concept called the 'functional principle'. Broadly speaking, this means that social problems are addressed on the basis of what the organisations can do as opposed to the nature of the problem and the needs of the client. The practical implementation of this is that agencies see clients in terms of the agency's key function. So, a housing department might see the need to house someone as their sole responsibility, but what if the person they are trying to help has a criminal record? What if they have an addiction to an illegal substance? These issues may impact upon their ability to retain their tenancy. From a very simple point of view, what if they offer an individual with an alcohol addiction a property right next door to an off-licence? Much better if the housing department in question can work with other agencies and their professionals to support the person so that their addiction and other related problems can be addressed in a holistic way. This is the logic of joint working.

However, increasingly since the late 1970s the unilateral approach came to be seen as inefficient largely because most people who need long-term social support have multiple problems which overlap the remit of different agencies. From around the beginning of the 1980s governments and organisational theorists started to see the need for a more co-ordinated approach to dealing with the clients of the state and as a result began pressing for a more joined-up approach to providing services (Ling, 2002; Cameron *et al.*, 2007). Arguably, the tragic sequence of child deaths that had agency failings, especially in the area of communication and joint working, at the heart of them only added momentum to the gradual movement away from the functional principle and opened the door for a more strategic and formalised joint working approach. Thus we have seen a continued growth in joined up working to the extent that it is almost mandatory for all new policies and processes to at least consider the impact of their actions on other organisations. In most areas this has gone further and joint working has become mandatory in many instances. In criminal justice terms, the three key examples are the Crime and Disorder Reduction Partnership, Community Safety Partnerships and the Drug and Alcohol Action Teams.

The need for and pitfalls in joint working: some examples

One group of people that regularly come to the attention of the criminal justice agencies are problematic drug users who are committing crimes on a regular basis to fund their drug use. Whilst at first glance it can be seen that offending behaviour would be of primary concern to the criminal justice system, it is worth noting that problematic illicit drug users can have some or all of the following problems as a direct result of their drug use:

• criminal offending behaviour to fund their drug consumption
• income problems due to an inability to work
• accommodation problems due to their chaotic life style and erratic income
• health problems as a direct result of their drug use and other associated illnesses
• child protection concerns
• the need for therapy/counselling for their drug use.

All of the above will impact on their offending behaviour, and addressing all of the above may significantly reduce the manner of their offending and the volume of crimes they commit.

As a result of these multiple problems, a single problematic drug user can be simultaneously in contact with the police, probation, local authority housing departments, an NHS General Practitioner, a specialist drug clinic, social services, a voluntary sector drug agency and probably the Department of Work and Pensions in order to claim some form of income support. In addition, as part of the new Coalition drug strategy it is likely that they will be in contact with some form of training agency trying to prepare them for work. Logistically manoeuvring around this wide-ranging set of agencies becomes difficult, especially if they are not working in a co-ordinated fashion.

Clearly, for both the client and at times the different agencies this causes confusion, duplication and a lack of coherence as each organisation will have their own agenda and policies for dealing with the client. Equally, each organisation will 'own' a part of the client's problem and also 'own' that particular intervention. For example, child protection has historically been the domain of social services, health-related needs that of the NHS and justice-related problems that of the courts, the police and probation. The result is often an incomplete service which at best leaves the client feeling frustrated, often misses the client's most pressing needs and at worst fails to adequately address their underlying root causes (Barton, 2002).

In addition, the extent of the complexity of workers and organisations involved with that client can and does lead to some mistakes being made. Local authorities have different departments for housing and social services; probation, the NHS and the police are separate from local authorities; each organisation uses different software and hardware, and so on and so on. We can see how the application of technology and the systems it creates and responds to can seem strange to external professionals – and indeed the general public – in the work of Innes (1999). In commenting on the findings of the Macpherson Report (1999), Innes outlines a project carried out over three years. The essence of his article questions the claim of Macpherson that the police service is institutionally racist, a subject we are not concerned with here. But, in laying out his concerns, he describes one of the criticisms that the Metropolitan Police Force failed to follow up leads and information quickly enough. However, at the time this was actually part of the process by which murder investigations were universally undertaken:

> It was [the] recognition that managing information was central to the activities performed by the police on major crime inquiries that led to the introduction of the Major Inquiry Standard Administrative Procedures (MIRSAP), subsequent to the criticisms made by Lord Byford responding to the failures within police systems in the hunt for the so-called 'Yorkshire Ripper', Peter Sutcliffe. MIRSAP established a protocol for the handling, use and storage of information collected by police as part of a major inquiry. As part of this, a specific division of labour was established within the inquiry team, between the strategic management of the inquiry, the officers tasked to conduct the investigative actions and the Major Incident Room which was responsible for the organisation and direction of investigative activities, as well as researching and analysing all incoming information. The objective behind this division of roles was

to establish a system that worked at optimal efficiency whilst minimising the potential for corruption and malfeasance by officers.

(Innes, 1999: 4.3)

The problem with this system was that it did not enable police investigations to filter the quality of information as it came in, which was then exacerbated by the data storage and retrieval system employed to build upon MIRSAP, the Home Office Large Major Enquiry System (HOLMES). What this example underlines is the very different approaches that criminal justice (let alone other public sector) agencies have for dealing with information, in terms of procedures and supporting technology, and the questionable logic implied by both.

The Soham murders of Holly Wells and Jessica Chapman by their school caretaker Ian Huntley in 2002 (for more detail and a timeline of events visit: http://news.bbc.co.uk/1/hi/england/2180946.stm) indicated that the problems identified by Innes in the conduct of murder investigations had not been adequately addressed, but also that significant gaps existed in the record-keeping of and the information sharing between different agencies and organisations (Bastable and Sheather, 2005). This is starkly exemplified in child protection cases such as the death of Victoria Climbié, where gaps in provision caused by agencies not working together were cited as a factor in Victoria's murder (Barton, 2002). Haringey was also the site of the case known as 'Baby P'. On 3 August 2007 Peter Connelly was found dead in his cot as a result of severe injuries, including a broken spine. He was 17 months old when he died; his injuries had been missed by doctors; he had been on the child protection register for the entire eight months he was being abused by his mother Tracey Connelly, his step-father Steven Barker and his brother Jason Owen. Peter suffered 50 injuries and was seen 60 times by different agencies involved with the family, yet nothing was done to protect him (Garboden, 2010). The review ordered by Ed Balls, then Secretary of State for Children, Schools and Families, carried out collaboratively by OFSTED, the Healthcare Commission and Her Majesty's Inspectorate of Constabularies (HMIC), found failures of strategic leadership, of planning and of front-line service provision, and that: 'Social care, health and police authorities do not communicate and collaborate routinely and consistently to ensure effective assessment, planning and review of cases of vulnerable children and young people' (OFSTED/ Healthcare Commission/HMIC, 2009: 3).

A brief word about core and peripheral tasks

At this stage, it is necessary for you to begin to understand the nature and lasting legacy of the 'functional principle' that dominated British public policy for so long. It created conditions where agencies and the professionals who work in them were almost forced to establish 'territory' and then ensure that they retained ownership of that territory. As a result, agencies developed what we can term 'core tasks'. These tasks then come to represent the main role of that organisation: diagnosis and prescription lie with doctors, detection and arrest with the police, child protection and family welfare with social workers, teachers education, and so on.

However, in addition to these core tasks, agencies also have to undertake what we can term 'peripheral' tasks. These are areas of work that are related to the organisation but may not quite fall into the core task. For example, teachers are charged with the education of their pupils; it is clearly their core task. But teachers also have some responsibility to watch for signs of child abuse and neglect, which, whilst important, is not part of their core task. The same is true for doctors: whilst their primary role is to diagnose and treat patients, they too have a role to play in child protection.

A more recent tension of this kind has emerged in the wake of the UK's part in propagating a 'War on Terror', where public sector professionals have been tasked with monitoring their client base for signs of terrorist sympathies or activities. Central in this debate has been the role of universities, as places where terrorist sympathies can be stimulated or reinforced. Certainly some Islamic groups with fundamental beliefs about Islam and its place in 'modern' Western societies have been active in targeting students as potential recruits (Briggs and Birdwell, 2009). This informed the UK government's Prevent strategy, which is partially designed to challenge radicalisation in UK universities. In many ways this follows a long-standing trend in government policy, which can be linked to the ongoing desire to invest public sector institutions and professionals with peripheral responsibilities for monitoring the immigration status of clients and users (Cohen, 2002a, 2002b; Humphries, 2004). There is evidence that in some institutions this peripheral responsibility is taken seriously, with a staff member and a student being arrested as a result of Nottingham University's security staff reporting them to the police for accessing a bomb-making manual used by al-Qaeda online, though for strictly academic purposes. Both were eventually released without charge (Townsend, 2012).

However, quite naturally, agencies and the professionals within them tend to see themselves and their work identities as married to their core tasks. Peripheral work comes behind core work in terms of resources and prioritisation of work-related planning. In the specific case of universities and the monitoring of staff and students, there has been resistance from within the sector; a lecturer at Nottingham University, Dr Rod Thornton, was suspended for criticising the treatment of the two arrestees. Such criticism has been echoed from without also, with Shami Chakrabarti, the Director of Liberty, asking: 'Is it right that universities are taking on policing duties?' (Townsend, 2011). Similarly, teachers do not always see themselves primarily as working in child protection and, importantly, neither does the public (Webb and Vulliamy, 2001). Thus we need to recognise the importance of core tasks not only for the professionals who work within agencies but also for the clients that are in receipt of their services.

Joint working in theory

Although joint working is mandatory in most instances, it takes various guises and happens in varying degrees. It is often dependent on the nature of the work, and it is true to say that the closer one gets to the core task of the agency, the less likely it is that joint working will take place. By way of illustration, if we take our problematic drug user as an example, it may be the case that the person is known by the courts and police to be a problematic drug user and has been identified as a suspect in a burglary case and needs to be arrested. The arrest will be effected by a police officer because that is one of the core tasks of the police. However, once the person has been charged and is in the custody cells, the police then may inform a drug support worker who will visit the drug user in the cells to assess their needs. Thus, by working together in this way both agencies assure that their core tasks become co-ordinated in an attempt to address the multiple needs of the client.

The best way to think about joint working is to imagine it along what social scientists call a continuum (or line) with the polar extremes of independence and merger (Crawford, 1995).

Figure 7.1 shows that the scope of joint working starts at one polar extreme with independence, where there is obviously no joint working at all, and ends at the polar opposite where organisations merge. If we consider this in terms of core tasks, it will be no surprise that the prison and probation arms of the system are moving ever closer.

Perhaps the simplest way to understand this as a theory is to think about how you may approach working towards assessments as a student. When you take examinations, you will do so independently as this represents your core task. As a result, whilst you may recognise the existence of other students in the room, there is no need or requirement to collaborate with them. You will plan and implement your own 'exam passing policy' with regard to researching the area, gathering information, revising and writing the exam paper.

When it comes to essay writing, you may wish to co-ordinate your work with other students and undertake some temporary collaboration. Of course, this will not go as far as writing the essays together (at least you really should not do this!), but it may be that you collaborate and share resources – books, articles, notes or whatever – in an attempt to be more efficient with your time and to avoid duplication. This will require some joint planning and some division of labour. In a perfect partnership you will identify tasks that require particular strengths and make sure that these are allocated to the most appropriate person.

| Independence | Coordination | Merger |

Figure 7.1 Joint-working continuum

However, where you have group elements to your assessments (which might include group presentations) in order to be successful you will need to undertake joint working – in effect you merge with other students into one new structure with a single identity. In a successful merger you will be able to plan together by setting short-term goals, identifying strengths and delegating responsibility within the policy goal of gaining the highest mark possible. Once the presentation is finished, you may disband the group and return to focusing on your core tasks, or you may keep a loose association and choose to work jointly again on other projects where joint working is required.

If we relate all that to organisations, you will see that the further away from the independence end of the continuum an organisation moves, the greater the threat to organisational independence and professional identity becomes. Once an organisation reaches the merger end of the continuum, organisational and professional identity is utterly lost. This is a dangerous place for agencies to be as it is possible that they will cease to exist and become part of a larger organisation without a separate identity or core task (Glatter, 2003).

Joint working in practice

There can be little doubt that in theory at least the policy of requiring agencies to work together is a good idea. However, given what we have already discussed in relation to implementation, it should be clear that making joint working happen is fraught with difficulties. There are two key reasons as to why joint working can be problematic: organisational resistance and professional identity. Organisations and the managers of organisations seek to retain their identity and control over their core business, to keep control over how resources are used and the ownership of a body of knowledge and expertise, and thus can see any call to work with another organisation as threatening to those aims. Professionals, as we have seen, are imbued with a workplace culture that provides them not only with the expertise to 'do the job' but also with a world view; for example, see Reiner (2000: chapter 3) and his work on 'cop culture'. As such, if we go back to our example of the problematic drug user, the same person at the same time will be known as a client, patient and offender, leading them to be viewed differently by the various professionals working with them.

Thus in practice joint working can be difficult. Hudson (1987) identifies three elements in joint working which can inhibit or facilitate good joint working.

1 The environmental context

Hudson notes a number of factors which may cause agencies to work together, ranging from a need to share resources to changes in policy. It is also important to add that since Hudson wrote up his research that environmental context now also includes mandated joint working, which in practice means that agencies now have very little choice as to whether they undertake joint working or not.

2 Comparative properties of the organisational network

Here Hudson is referring to the similarities and differences in terms of organisations. He suggests that the more similar agencies are, in terms of working practices, ideologies, recognising and respecting the boundaries of other agencies' strengths and weaknesses, being aware of the presence of other agencies, having the ability to reciprocate in resource exchanges so that the transfer of resources is not one way leading to resentment, and the presence or absence of alternative partners, the more effectively they will work jointly.

3 Collaborative linkages

This refers to the manner in which organisations 'do' joint working. Hudson argues that the more formal and rule bound the partnership is, if there is the presence of a co-ordinating body, if there are mutual exchanges of resources and mutual respect between the organisations and the professionals and if there are standardised protocols between organisations, then the more likely it is that organisations will work together.

In practice it is very unusual to find all those factors in one partnership forum. The reality is that some organisations are more powerful than others and tend to dominate joint working arrangements. This is sometimes aided by government policy. For example, problematic drug users who are committing crimes to fund their use are generally both persistent criminals whose offending needs to be addressed and suffering from drug-related illnesses. This means that both the criminal justice system and the medical profession could lay claim to ownership of the 'drug problem' and both could lay equal claim to being the 'lead' agency. However, Barton (2011) notes that in the past twenty years the needs of the criminal justice system have been key in shaping and driving illicit drug policy due to the political need to be 'tough on crime'.

The New Labour government arguably laid the strongest foundations for dealing with offenders in a joined-up way by implementing the Integrated Offender Management (IOM) system (Senior *et al.*, 2011). This was operational from 2009 onwards and was designed to target the most persistent and damaging offenders in different areas through effective partnership working. Although each locality is able to co-ordinate their own tailored response according to local circumstances and context, there are strong actions that have to be observed and the IOMs were expected to (Home Office, 2010: 2):

- reduce crime, reduce re-offending and improve public confidence in the criminal justice system;
- address potential overlaps between existing approaches and programmes to manage offenders and address gaps;
- align the work of local criminal justice agencies, expanding and improving on partnerships that already exist at the local, area and regional level with wider social agendas;

- simplify and strengthen governance, to provide greater clarity around respective roles and responsibilities – including leadership, operational decision making and allocation of resources.

It is perhaps too early to evaluate the outcomes of the system, particularly with a change of government into the bargain, but there have been early claims of success. A survey carried out on behalf of the Home Office indicates that implementation has been achieved in many areas, and that, while barriers exist, partnerships are being formed (though more could be done to include voluntary and third-sector organisations), and there is evidence of efficiency gains (see the executive summary here: http://www.homeoffice.gov.uk/publications/ crime/reducing-reoffending/IOM-Survey-Exec-Summary?view=Binary). A more recent process evaluation of five of the six pioneer sites suggests that more needs to be done in terms of clearly defining IOM partnerships, crafting truly localised responses and encouraging partnerships to develop beyond the boundaries of existing structures (Senior *et al.*, 2011).

Successive government policies have prioritised the criminal justice element of such partnerships, thus ensuring that criminal justice organisations and concerns dominate joint working in areas such as the illicit drug field. Equally, vast sums of money have been poured into the criminal justice system, which meant that very often the partner agencies became the poor relations. However, while the police in particular were protected, as we set out above, this has clearly changed, with an overall loss in funding of £3 billion, meaning a 20 per cent budget reduction for the police service and a 23 per cent reduction across the areas covered by the Ministry of Justice. Ultimately 37,000 job losses are predicted, with funding for street policing secured until 2013, but there are to be closures of courts and prisons (despite rising prisoner numbers and some new prisons coming on line) and disruptions to probation services are already occurring as we write (Travis, 2011). The impact of such far-reaching and severe reductions in expenditure, coupled with the loss of human resources and experience, on the future of joint working is something that will only become clear in the fullness of time.

Conclusion

This has been a very brief excursion into what is an important and expanding area of policy formulation and implementation. It would be impossible to provide full information in a single chapter and if this is an area that interests you, there are numerous specialist textbooks you can refer to. That said, there are some key points concerning joint working that you need to be aware of:

- Joint working has become the norm and is integral to government planning. It is rare that any new policy will be formulated and implemented without at least considering joint working.
- In theory, joint working can be formulated and implemented relatively straightforwardly.

- Organisational and professional resistance can act to block joint working in practice.
- In many instances joint working does not extend very far beyond the co-ordination/integration stage, as going any further along the continuum poses a threat to organisational independence and identity.
- One notable exception in the criminal justice system is the implementation of an Integrated Offender Management system, but how effective this will be in the long term remains to be seen.
- Given the current austerity measures introduced by the Coalition government, it is difficult to predict how joint working, with all of the obstacles that generally exist, will develop.

Questions for consideration

1. What do you understand by the term 'functional principle'? How might this impact on policy delivery in complex situations?
2. Looking at the police, can you identify their 'core task'? How does the core task determine their role in society?
3. In dealing with a problematic drug user who is also a prolific and persistent offender, which agency should take the lead role and why?

8   Auditing, evaluating and managing policy implementation

Introduction

It should be clear from reading the previous chapters that there is generally a gap between the formulation and implementation of policy. As a result of this, there is a very good chance that the policy aims of the politicians can be subverted or undermined by the actions of street level bureaucrats, which can have serious implications for both longer-term future political success and the shorter-term aim of achieving specific policy-related goals. As a result, policy makers and politicians need to be sure that the tasks they set for those who implement policy are being achieved in the desired manner. Of equal importance, if not more important in many ways, is the question of obtaining value for money. The government invests billions of pounds of tax payers' money in the criminal justice system on an annual basis and it, as well as the taxpayers, need to be assured that the money is used with a large degree of fiscal probity.

As a result of these twin sets of pressures and needs, governments have always attempted to audit and evaluate what service-delivery organisations are doing with the aim of ensuring they are delivering services in an appropriate manner. However, the nature and direction of audit, evaluation and management have undergone a radical transformation in the past twenty years, which has had a significant impact on the way in which criminal justice organisations go about their daily business. We can be quite specific as to when this happened – if you recall, in chapter 3 we discussed the changes which took place in the political, economic and social landscape of Britain during the late 1970s and through the 1980s, and it is to that period of British political and policy development that we now return.

The genesis of change

Many different labels have been applied to the changes that occurred in Britain during the 1980s. Here is not the place to discuss or debate which label is correct. For our purposes, we view this political era as being largely inspired by free-market liberals who were ideologically opposed to any form of state intervention, combined with the seemingly paradoxical influence of neo-conservatives who emphasised a strong state maintaining a 'traditional' moral order (Levitas, 1986; Marchak, 1991; George and Wilding, 1994, etc.). Clearly, given the centrality of the state and state agencies to the running of complex Western nations, it was impossible for politicians to fully implement the ideas of the free-market liberals as they conceived them, particularly with the added drag factor of neo-conservatism. However, as we set out previously, the British government, led by Margaret Thatcher (who in turn was heavily influenced by people like Keith Joseph, himself a keen disciple of the economist Milton Friedman), was so convinced of the supposed shortcomings of the state that they undertook a comprehensive overhaul of British society with the aim of introducing many of the free-market principles espoused by Friedman and his acolytes. This wave of Friedman-inspired change was not restricted to Britain: the Chicago School (so-called because it was based at the University of Chicago) of which Friedman was a leading light wielded enormous influence in spreading liberal economic ideas. In some countries, such as Chile, the adoption of free-market principles can almost be seen as quasi-experimental, with Friedman claiming that the 'economic miracle' there was comparable with the success of countries such as Germany and Japan in the post-war period. Of course, there are divergent interpretations of the Chilean experiment and its outcomes (Klein, 1989) but there can be little doubt about its far-reaching effects.

It is worth taking a small diversion here to underline the degree of importance these theories were given by their followers in Britain. Ian Gilmour (1992: 17), who served in the Cabinet under Margaret Thatcher, had this to say about the extent to which Friedman's theories were regarded as flawless, such that:

> admissions of doubt or ignorance would have been inappropriate intruders into Friedman's theorizing. He was not, after all, putting forward a hypothesis or just another theory. His theory was infallibly true; it was both faith and science ... For Friedman, a theory which evidently combined every known virtue provided a complete economic system and a political ideology as well. As for Friedman, so for his Thatcherite followers.

It is worth keeping in mind the certainty with which the successive Thatcher governments went about introducing their changes: these were not experiments, rather they were certainties. There could be no argument that their vision was correct and each and every other vision was wrong, as Mrs Thatcher stressed in defending the record of her administrations, particularly in leading the way in Europe and beyond:

> During the past 11 years, this Government have had a clear and unwavering vision of the future of Europe and Britain's role in it. It is a vision which stems from our deep-seated attachment to parliamentary democracy and commitment to economic liberty, enterprise, competition and a free market economy. No Government in Europe have fought more resolutely against subsidies, state aids to industry and protectionism; unnecessary regulation

and bureaucracy and increasing unaccountable central power at the expense of national Parliaments. No Government have fought more against that in Europe than we have ... We have worked for our vision of a Europe which is free and open to the rest of the world, and above all to the countries of eastern Europe as they emerge from the shadows of socialism. It would not help them if Europe became a tight-knit little club, tied up in regulations and restrictions. They deserve a Europe where there is room for their rediscovered sense of nationhood and a place to decide their own destiny after decades of repression.

(http://www.margaretthatcher.org/document/108256)

Thus, from the outset, everything about the state, but especially where the state intervened in the market – areas such as welfare, housing, education, health and so on – was either immoral or inefficient or both. The optimum manner in which to run people's lives was to allow the market and market machinery to take over. As a result, from the early 1980s, managers were presented by some leading Conservative figures as virtually the saviours of the nation: 'efficient management is the key to the [national] revival ... and the management ethos must run right through our national life – private and public companies, nationalised industries, local government, the National Health Service' (Heseltine, 1980, quoted in Clarke and Newman, 1997: 34).

Having alerted you to the fact that these changes were undertaken with an almost missionary-like zeal, we can delve a little deeper into the history of the changes. The starting point for this journey can be located in a growing dissatisfaction with the traditional running of the British post-war welfare state, specifically the heavily bureaucratised process of social administration.

Far from being the embodiment of full citizenship, as T.H. Marshall (1950) believed then, the welfare state was regarded by the New Right as infantilising, reducing individuals to the status of children. We talked earlier about the desire of policy makers to secure their policy goals, and the street level bureaucracy that forms part of an ongoing implementation gap. For the Conservatives under Margaret Thatcher, a key role in the damage wrought on British society was played by the professionals responsible for delivering welfare services. From a position of unparalleled trust where certain professionals, in particular clinicians, actually determined the parameters of policy (Klein, 1989), state employed (and often trained) welfare professionals saw their stock plummet dramatically and in a relatively short period of time. As Foster and Wilding (2000: 144) point out, professionalism was under fire from different political directions, but the Conservatives were in a position to formulate policy:

The charge from the New Right was that professionally dominated services like the NHS were always unresponsive to patients because there were no built-in incentives to put clients' needs first. They were monopolies lacking the essential stimulus of competition. They were also wasteful of resources because professionals, like bureaucrats, were self-interested budget maximizers rather than altruistic servants of their clients and the common good.

In the colourful imagery of Julian Le Grand, welfare professionals slipped from knights to knaves in the political and popular consciousness (Le Grand, 1997). Only in a free market supported by a facilitative state could individuals express their autonomy and secure optimal welfare outcomes.

Another key determinant in questioning the control and delivery of welfare was the fiscal crisis of the early 1970s, which gave rise to a search for the commitment to lower taxation and the need of 'sound stewardship' of scarce public funds (O'Connor, 2002). To put it bluntly, then, as now, it was seen by some that the British state was unable to continue to pay for substantial state investment in the provision of welfare and that budget cuts needed to be made. Again, then as now, this was driven by changes in the nature of global capitalism.

By 1973 the nature of capitalism had undergone changes which economists call *structural*, in respect of the depth of reform required to place wealth accumulation back on an even keel. In the 1970s this was principally caused by an oil price and supply crisis. As a result of these structural changes, conditions were created where the nature of all aspects of economic production and social organisation were placed under closer scrutiny. Thus, in the context of Britain, the Beveridge–Keynesian axis, with its emphasis on demand economics, full employment and a relatively benevolent welfare regime, was seen as a blocking agent to the economic restructuring required if Britain was to compete in the emerging 'global economy'.

What was it, then, about the Beveridge–Keynesian axis which made it a 'blocking agent'? It is possible to view the Beveridge–Keynesian approach to welfare as a product of its time. James and Raine (1998), looking at the growth of managerialism in criminal justice agencies, note that the post-war welfare state was created in the mould of existing models of production and control and was centred around the need to reconstruct British society in the aftermath of war. They suggest that the blueprint for the new welfare state was the Fordist model of production with its emphasis on uniformity and bulk production. Control of this 'welfare production line' was handed over to administrators who were charged with delivering reliable and consistent services. This was achieved by employing bureaucrats – the welfare state's equivalent of production-line operatives – who 'produced' welfare services via task specification, hierarchical command, co-ordination of information and segmented structures.

The result was the creation of a post-war welfare state which was 'standardised and consistent' (James and Raine, 1998: 32) but without flexibility and certainly not able to respond to the needs of the user. In the 1960s this was dramatically underlined as poverty was 'rediscovered' and the role of state welfare in slaying the giants identified by Beveridge was called seriously into question (Lowe, 1995). Indeed, by the mid-1970s the welfare bureaucracies were under attack for being too self-obsessed, too profligate with public money and failing to meet the needs of the service users (Clarke and Newman, 1997). The first Thatcher government drove an attack on the power bases of bureau-professionals, drawing on such tactics as fiscal constraint, compulsory competitive tendering, internal fragmentation of organisations into separate agencies, and a move from explanatory and co-operative accountability towards calculative and contractual accountability. Other shifts included the introduction of performance targets, indicators and measurement (Carter, 1989). In short, the new regime was aimed at eliminating wasteful duplication by streamlining welfare delivery and introducing market discipline.

Central to the changes to the nature of the welfare state was a greater emphasis on fiscal probity and economic control of 'wasteful' organisations. In turn this gave rise to the prominence of the concept of the three 'Es': economy, efficiency and effectiveness. The Audit Commission (1983: para. 36) defined these concepts as follows:

- *Economy* may be defined as the terms under which the authority acquires human and material resources. An economical operation acquires those resources in the appropriate quality and quantity at the lowest cost.

- *Efficiency* may be defined as the relationship between goods and services produced and the resources used to produce them. An efficient operation produces the maximum output for a given set of resource outputs; or, it has minimum inputs for any given quantity and quality of service provided.

- *Effectiveness* may be defined as how well a programme or activity is achieving its established goals or other intended benefits.

Thus, this first tranche of changes set about ensuring that state agencies were aware of and working under a need to produce services that had 'value for money'. At the time this process was linked to the idea of 'hollowing out the state' at a conceptual level. On a more practical, outcomes-oriented, level the 'success' of 'Thatcherism' in achieving greater economy, efficiency and effectiveness has been roundly disputed (see Rhodes, 1994).

However, there was a second aspect of change which revolved around the contentious (and ideological) area of which system of control is more 'effective' in the delivery and running of welfare agencies – bureau-professional control or managerial control?

The dissatisfaction with the bureau-professional control of welfare agencies

It is not necessary to enter into a prolonged debate concerning the problems with the bureaucratic control of welfare. It is, however, necessary to point out that, accompanying the drive towards greater fiscal probity, was the idea that the bureau-professionals who were running the post-war welfare state from its inception until 1979 were not the best group of people to be entrusted with ensuring the required economic rigour. For example, it has been argued that professionals are 'seduced' by professional rewards and thus 'lose sight' of how their consumers actually experience a service. This propelled the suspicion that welfare provision was for the benefit of its deliverer and not its receiver, to reiterate the analysis of Le Grand (1997) above that welfare professionals were knaves more often than knights. Essentially, what was being argued was that the old-style control and accountability practices of the Beveridge–Keynesian welfare state were unable or unwilling to make the adjustments to their standard operating procedures (Hill, 2005) needed to facilitate the change to a flexible and 'consumer friendly' form of welfare delivery which could actively promote and foster a climate that embraced the concepts of economy, efficiency and effectiveness. Thus, the search was on for a new form of control and delivery, one that ensured that the practices and beliefs of the market-driven private sector were transferred into the public sector.

Enter New Public Management (NPM), the phrase used to describe the incursion of private sector values into the management of public sector agencies, revolving around increasing accountability and promoting best practice. Therefore, this change had two dimensions regarding the reform of welfare. Firstly, it was concerned with providing strategic leadership and direction for organisations. In many ways this vision of management mirrors that of Heseltine, cited above. Managers are often seen as 'heroic' or 'bold' and are able to inspire their workforce to 'commitment to the organisational missions' (Clarke and Newman, 1997: 3). Thatcher and Reagan have been credited with promoting this through a focus on management as a dimension of a new enterprise culture. Interestingly, it may be that the emphasis on private sector ideas has in the longer term served to undermine managers in public settings, as consultants and 'gurus' have gained significant purchase over managerial practice (Clark and Salaman, 1998). Certainly the authors of this book have experienced through contracted research the influence that consultants have in certain public agencies (although it may be that this extends only as far as institutional needs require).

Secondly, NPM allows for the devolution of responsibility from the centre with an increased importance for local managers who are 'close' to their 'customers'. This allows devolution of responsibility to the local level, but importantly it enables local managers to feed into the strategic thinking because they are 'in tune' with the needs of the client group. There is a large literature dedicated to more effectively responding to local needs through proximity and identification, and this has been a very big part of the process of trying to improve services to Black and Minority Ethnic (BME) groups. In essence, one of the ways in which the specific needs of BME communities might be met is through diversifying front-line staff and management teams (Johns, 1999; Lorbiecki and Jack, 2000; Rowe, 2004, 2007). However, attempting to 'empower' different groups through devolving power can create conflict between those seeking to provide and those who receive services (Peters and Pierre, 2000). Indeed, in the context of policing in the United States where police personnel – including at the level of middle management – in diverse areas have been shaped to reflect the demographic profile of their service populations, the outcomes have been detrimental in many ways (Walker *et al.*, 2003).

This introduces two connected and important elements into NPM. Firstly, NPM can be conceived of as an ideology inasmuch as there is a belief that managers will somehow always be successful; this belies the fact that numerous private enterprises go into liquidation every year despite being headed up by managers. Looking at the retail sector alone in 2011, 31 companies failed, impacting on over 24,000 employees (see http://www.retailresearch.org/whosegonebust.php). There is also an assumption that 'managers' are intrinsically better at making decisions than bureaucrats. For Margaret Thatcher there may even have been a religious dimension to this, a Christian-influenced management reflecting a belief in inspired leadership in line with the moral and social revolution she sought to introduce (Pattinson, 1997). It has to be noted, then, that this promotion of managers over bureaucrats is often not based in anything other than belief – there is, as far as we are aware, no extensive body of evidence to support this perspective.

Secondly, NPM becomes a practice inasmuch as it is a practical way of dealing with problematic sections of society. This is achieved by altering public provision so as to allow the recipients of state intervention scope for things such as choice, flexibility and a more tailored approach to the services they receive. Choice has become a key issue for public services, with commentators like Le Grand (1991) arguing for some time that not only is choice desirable but the best mechanism for achieving policy outcomes. In fact, he has stated that choice within public provision will act as 'the other invisible hand' for the public sector, mirroring its operation in the free market (Le Grand, 2007). The practical manifestation of this was to introduce a raft of changes across some of the main areas of public provision.

One of the most important of these was the implementation of so-called quasi or internal markets, and the National Health Service was perhaps the key policy area in which this was implemented; for an early and insightful discussion of the health care context see Enthoven (1991). Without going into too much detail, which is unnecessary for our purposes, the idea was to introduce competition and choice by separating the responsibility for commissioning services from the responsibility for providing them:

> Although its activities continue to be paid for out of general taxation [the NHS], salary deductions, and, to a much smaller extent, user-charges, their efficiency is determined, at least in theory, by a strict purchaser/provider split modelled on the split between buyer and seller on the open market. In theory, providers compete for patients, and the competition, at least at the level of hospitals, drives down prices and raises the quality and supply of treatment. Prices are also supposed to be driven down by freeing up the labour-market in health care, allowing savings to be made according to regional variations in the cost of living and rates of unemployment.

For the system to work as intended, the costs of labour and capital and the effectiveness of treatment need to be monitored in great detail, and measures of performance have to be agreed and widely adopted.

(Sorrell, 1997: 71–2)

Thus choice and competition as drivers of change had to be supported by clear and coherent measurements of performance.

These attempts have been subject to criticism both in theory and in practice. Doubts were expressed about the motives for internal market policies, that the changes are driven more by a desire to reduce public expenditure than to improve service quality (Sorrell, 1997). Despite embracing many of the managerialist priorities of their Conservative predecessors, New Labour was less committed to the idea of internal markets, preferring to emphasise 'partnerships' as a natural supplement to competition in public provision (Cutler and Waine, 2000). Furthermore, choice, particularly as promoted by Le Grand, has received significant criticism, most recently from Hunter (2009), who suggests that the determination of New Labour to operationalise choice and competition runs counter to the evidence, which was puzzling for a government wedded to the idea of evidence-based policy making.

It is important to be aware of these debates because they have had such far-reaching implications for public policy in the UK. Of course, the internal market had relatively little relevance for the criminal justice system, where privatisation was largely limited for a long time to the building and running of prisons. This has gradually changed over time (Jones and Garland, 2005; Button *et al.*, 2007) and, as we write in the context of swingeing cuts in the budgets of public sector organisations, certain police services have caused controversy by considering privatising some elements of their operations. West Midlands and Surrey police invited private companies to bid for contracts to provide a variety of support services, including detaining suspects, neighbourhood patrols and criminal investigations. Predictably there have been varied reactions to this development, with the *Daily Mail* underlining the potential for freeing police officers to be present on the streets (Slack, 2012) and commentators in the *Guardian* expressing concerns about the impartiality of policing and the problems of sponsorship more widely (Travis and Jowit, 2012). How this plays out in practice will be interesting to monitor, though arguing, as a senior officer did in supporting the changes, that private security is already a feature of UK society seems a little problematic.

By way of summary it is possible to suggest that those shifts had two areas of impact. Firstly, criminal justice organisations needed to alter their own world views and standard operating procedures in order to accommodate the move towards a 'managerial state' (Clarke and Newman, 1997; Crawford and Newburn, 2002). Secondly, those individuals who switched from bureau-professionals to being new public managers had to change the way they conceived of their work and, importantly for this chapter, how they demonstrated policy 'success'. One way was to increase the use of audit and evaluation.

Audit and evaluation – the use of Key Performance Indicators to control professionals

Over the last twenty-five years those working in the public sector will have found it difficult, if not impossible, to escape what Power (1997) refers to as the audit explosion. Whilst in the private sector the principal purpose of auditing has been to check for financial probity, in the public sector this function has gradually been surpassed by other forms of audit. Under the Conservative governments of the 1980s and 1990s there was a strong focus on the use of audit to secure greater economy and efficiency. Under New Labour this continued, and was arguably intensified, crystallising in the current role of audit in the identification and promotion of best practice. Given the changing focus of audit, it is important that you are aware of the role of audit as an agent for individual and organisational change.

Clarke *et al.* (2000) suggest that this change in audit from one of checking for probity towards being a method of change and control is a result of two factors. Firstly, it emanates from what we discussed above: a growing discourse of mistrust about the alleged self-interest and profligacy of public sector bureau-professionals, who have become disconnected from their once-accepted claims of public service. This discourse originates from both the right and the left of the political spectrum, although with the rise of neo-liberalism the right's voice has been the more politically influential. Secondly, auditing presents itself as a potential solution to the problem of controlling a mixed economy approach, as the co-ordination of social life, including the work and employees of the criminal justice system, has become spread across a mixed economy of finance, provision and regulation.

The contribution of the audit process to this problem of control over untrustworthy bureau-professionals and dispersed power and influence lies in its ability to perform as an 'industry of comfort production' (Power, 1997: 147). Because of its alleged capacity to 'see through what are often hidden practices, and through its claim to independence and neutrality, it seeks to deliver trust and measurement' (Clarke, 2004). Actually, if we focus on trust as an issue, there has been a decline in public belief in politics and politicians, with Burnham *et al.* (2008) charting levels of trust between 1983 and 2009. In this period it reached an all-time low of 13 per cent in 2009, which is perhaps unsurprising given the issues around corruption and the expenses scandals at this time. Comparatively trust in criminal justice professionals remained high, with the police hovering around 60 per cent and judges receiving higher ratings at the end of the period at 80 per cent. This seems ironic as welfare and criminal justice professionals have been subject to political doubts about their trustworthiness. For those of you who would like to review the issue of trust more fully see Seldon (2010) and Johns *et al.* (2012).

Under the New Labour government, which was seemingly obsessed with a focus on a 'what works' approach to new projects, the audit process created a situation in which the value of audit, and its ability to provide 'facts' about organisational behaviour, became an almost unassailable orthodoxy. Even though, as Hunter (2009) maintained, the willingness to be led by the evidence gathered through such activities seemed to be less apparent. What this focus on 'what works' appears to do is to conceal the ideological perspectives of those making policy; it suggests that there is a 'truth' operating freely from subjective world views. While we would not advocate the idea that truths are relative or a matter of construction and discourse, we do accept that truths are interpreted through the lens of our own perspectives. In policymaking, advocating 'what works' is arguably a particularly dangerous position to adopt as it can amount to dishonesty at worst, and at best may pave the way for serious unintended consequences. As we have argued elsewhere (Barton and Johns, 2005) in exploring the 'common sense' approach of New Labour, one person's attack on multiculturalism is another's open doorway to usher in 'new' forms of racism.

Given the rise in the perceived value of audit and following the political changes outlined above, the government set about ensuring that state organisations adhered more closely to the demands of their political masters. As we have seen, this is important because of the implementation gap. To put this simply, politicians had too much to lose if their policies were subverted at street level and so needed to devise ways in which they could (a) ensure that their policies were being implemented in the manner in which they were formulated and (b) introduce some form of control over street level bureaucrats. With those two ends in mind, they turned to the Audit Commission and the use of Key Performance Indicators (KPIs). KPIs are essentially a list of targets and objectives against which performance over a stated period of time is measured (for those of you who are interested, you can see the Devon and Cornwall police's 'performance against targets' report at www.devon-cornwall.police.uk/ v3/publrep/AnnualPolicingStratPlan/13performance.html).

Virtually all public sector agencies have KPIs and they are required to produce annual reports which measure their successes or failures in reaching them. The KPIs themselves are usually set by central government and reflect the aims and direction of their policies and as such are liable to change. For example, a couple of years ago the government showed a concern over the rise in violent crime. As a result the police were asked to focus their efforts on reducing such crimes. Failure to do so would mean that the police managers would face censure and perhaps dismissal. Thus managers are under pressure to ensure that those beneath them prioritise work which is covered by the KPIs.

In some respects this is a good move as it ensures that policy is implemented in the manner in which it is intended and not subverted by the personal preferences of street level bureaucrats. However, questions have been asked about the transformative power of the KPIs as, in practice, only work which is covered by the KPIs gets prioritised and other work, which may be of equal importance, gets neglected as no credit is given for it. For example, the primary KPI for prisons is that no prisoners should escape. In some respects this can be seen to be the correct focus; however, critics have claimed that the prioritising of security has led to a decline in rehabilitation and a rise in repeat offending (Solomon, 2004). The police service, constrained by the performance culture established by the government, Her Majesty's Inspectorate of Constabulary (HMIC) and the Audit Commission (Long, 2003), has responded with some enthusiasm, although Loveday (2000) has pointed to the way in which police managers have allowed service priorities to be distorted in some cases by the KPIs. Bird *et al.* (2005: 1), in reporting the outcomes of a Working Party on Performance Monitoring in the Public Services in 2003, recognised the value of performance measures but also stated that: '[Performance monitoring] done well is broadly productive for those concerned. Done badly, it can be very costly and not merely ineffective but harmful and indeed destructive.'

What this illustrates is the potential for measures and targets to create perverse incentives in some cases to neglect areas that are difficult to measure, but which might be more important. At the heart of this also is the continuing tension that exists between politicians/policy makers and service providers and the difficulty of creating meaningful universal standards that are flexible enough to reflect the skills of professionals in the specific contexts in which they are needed.

Conclusion

Management, audit and evaluation have become an integral part of the policy process within the criminal justice system. As a result we have seen a more centralised, if somewhat more devolved, method of controlling the activities of the street level bureaucrats. Central government policy makers have devised systems which enable them to ensure not only that their priorities are being met but also that there is a direct form of accountability from street level to Home Secretary.

There are, however, a couple of problems. First, there is a possibility that only work which is measured gets prioritised. This can lead to a lack of professional discretion and autonomy, which in turn can lead, for example, to 'policing by numbers' rather than the exercise of common sense. Secondly, whilst economy and efficiency can be objectively quantified – they can be measured using recognised formulae – 'effectiveness' is subjective and any debate about 'what works' will be shaped by the ideological foundation of the evaluator. Just as Easton (1953, cited in Hill, 1997) pointed to the normative nature of problem identification, so judging effectiveness will depend upon the value positions of those tasked with making such judgements.

Questions for consideration

1. What do you understand by the terms 'manager' and 'bureaucrat'? Critically discuss any differences between the two.
2. Can the criminal justice agencies be run on business-like approaches? What might be the costs and benefits of passing policing responsibilities on to private and third-sector actors?
3. In what ways might audit and KPIs restrict the autonomy of the professionals working within criminal justice organisations?

9 Equal opportunities and policing
A policy case study

Introduction

This chapter is designed to pick up on the themes, models and issues outlined in the earlier sections of the book and breathe some more life into them. Equal opportunities legislation and policy provide a really nice case when looked at through the lens of the criminal justice system. In order to keep it manageable, we will focus on the period New Labour were in office, 1997–2010, largely because they placed equality of opportunity at the centre of their political agenda, but also because they had the perfect vehicle to apply their principles in the criminal justice system in the shape of the Macpherson Report (1999). The report became a much larger critique of the system and the deep-rooted problems of institutional racism, but it started life as an investigation into police processes and for this reason (coupled with the desire to remain realistic) we will concentrate on equal opportunities and policing. What this example gives us is an insight into the real-world problems that impact upon policy making in practice.

To add another dimension to things, we will employ the framework established by Hall (1993) to evaluate whether what New Labour tried to achieve was a paradigmatic change in the criminal justice system, or alternatively simply about altering settings or instruments. This has particular relevance for the criminal justice system because of the historical problems it has had in appearing to be fair and just towards all sections of society. Policing has certainly been at the heart of such problems, with 'Nigger hunting in England', a report published by Hunte in 1965, vividly portraying the extent and nature of the discrimination experienced by minority ethnic communities. Furthermore, as Bowling and Phillips (2003: 529) recount in a review of the area, it has remained at the heart of 'race relations' in the UK:

> Research on policing conducted in the 1970s, 1980s and early 1990s indicated that racism and racial prejudice in police culture were more widespread and more extreme than in wider society. Studies found that 'racial prejudice and racialist talk ... [were] pervasive ... expected, accepted and even fashionable' (Smith and Gray, 1985: 388–89) while

negative views of people from ethnic minorities and support for extreme right political parties were widespread.

It is also important because of the limited impact equal opportunities had made on elements of criminal justice right up to the point that Labour were elected in 1997. As with every other chapter in this book, all we can offer here is a brief introduction to a massively complicated issue; however, discussing equal opportunities in this way is quite innovative and will enable you to explore the subject in more detail if you choose to do so.

Summarising New Labour and the third way

As a starting point, it is worth reflecting on the background and political ideals of New Labour. They came to power having shifted the party away from the left of British politics towards the centre, taking a new stance on 'social democracy' (Johns *et al.*, 2010; for fuller accounts of this transformation see Heffernan, 2001). One of the interesting things about New Labour from a policy-making point of view is that they claimed to have no ideology, no set of normative beliefs to guide their policy-making agenda (Powell, 2000; Newman, 2001). Reflecting back on what we said in chapter 3, ideology is a key factor in the creation and implementation of policy. Many commentators have treated the New Labour claim with a high degree of scepticism:

> What is lamentable about Blair's reported view is not the 'fact' that it ostensibly announces but the illusion it promotes. Marx held ideology to be dissimulative, a distortion of the relations of the material world. Now, however, we are more likely to contend that a declared disavowal of ideology is a colossal act of self-deception. Forty years ago, the shaking off of ideology and the proclamation of its death reflected the confidence of the Western world in the converging economic and social policies encouraged by states and governments propelled by Keynesian theories. Since then, it has become necessary not to abandon ideology but to look for it in more subtle, and frequently more fragmented, manifestations.
>
> (Freeden, 1999: 42)

Additionally, the dangers of denying the existence of ideological influences have been identified in different contexts, not least the potential of legitimating sophisticated forms of racism flagged up by the authors of this book (Barton and Johns, 2005). Whether there is any validity in the claim, however, the reality is that the perception shaped the way in which policy was presented.

Different commentators have tried to sum up the New Labour programme in different ways. For Julian Le Grand (1998) it could be described using the acronym CORA:

- Community
- Opportunity

- Responsibility
- Accountability.

While we might see equality of opportunity fitting the 'opportunity' component of this framework most clearly, it also connects to the other strands. What New Labour were interested in predominantly were communities of identity, initially based in 'race' and ethnicity but then moving out to incorporate age, sexuality and religion. Located in the wider framework, opportunity was conceived of as the flip side of responsibility, where rebalancing rights with responsibilities through the application of communitarian thinking meant that individuals had a right to expect state-facilitated opportunities (like freedom from discrimination) but that they then had responsibilities to make the most of those opportunities. Finally, in order to work at all equality of opportunity requires constant monitoring and evaluation. Those profile questions – 'what is your age/religion/ethnic background?' – that many people detest are seen as the lifeblood of ensuring an end to discrimination (Jewson *et al.*, 1992). Accountability is a necessary part of pursuing greater equality of opportunity. There are alternative conceptions of course; Lister (1998) preferred Responsibility, Inclusion and Opportunity (RIO), while Powell (2000) refers to PAP, short for pragmatism and populism, and these alternative conceptual frameworks seem equally relevant and useful. However, for the sake of argument CORA arguably fits the commitment to (obsession with?) equal opportunities that New Labour displayed.

Some might regard frameworks like this as the core components of an ideology, but this was not the way in which New Labour presented its approach (Fairclough, 2000). Removing ideology from the equation left a desire to apply 'common sense', which was about doing 'what works' rather than trying to create a utopia based on a preconceived political programme (Lister, 2001). In order to operationalise this common-sense project the previous government emphasised the importance of basing policy making on evidence (Solesbury, 2001). The pragmatism identified by Powell (2000) derives from this stated desire to make effective policy on the strength of the best available information.

In this aim they conformed very firmly with the rational model of policy making that we described in chapter 6. Invoking common sense suggests that there are social problems that would be recognised by any rational actor; having successfully identified such problems, the next phase is to understand them fully in order to formulate an effective response or responses, and this is where the application of existing evidence comes into play. Under New Labour there was an emphasis on review techniques, including systematic reviews and rapid evidence assessments (Barton, 2002). Where evidence was not already available, research was commissioned.

In this policy-making agenda we can see the rational model (see Figure 9.1). As we saw previously, there have been several critiques of the rational model, not least that it does not truly reflect policy making at all. It ignores the

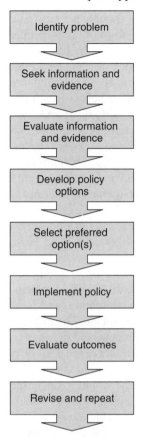

Figure 9.1 Rational policy making

ideological influences, the impact of policy ghosts (what went before) and the many hurdles that are thrown up in the shift from design to implementation, including the role of actors at the coalface of policy (street level bureaucrats). For many, the incremental model is a much more realistic account of how policy is conceived, designed, implemented, evaluated and revised, and in the discussion below of how equality of opportunity was pushed forward in the criminal justice context this will perhaps become more apparent. However, before we get to that point, it is important to explore the claim that New Labour were committed to drawing the curtains down once and for all on the centrality of political ideology.

Equal opportunities, New Labour and ideology

Equal opportunities measures actually allow us to unpick the claims of New Labour that they were merely applying common sense. In truth, very little is known about public opinion where the value of equal opportunities as a policy matter is concerned, though a recent survey of 3,000 potential UK voters by the Fabian Society found that 94 per cent of the respondents felt no one should face discrimination on the basis of disability. Similarly, there was clear and overwhelming support for greater equality of opportunity, especially relating to the equality strands of age and socio-economic status (Jolley, 2007). However, supporting the belief that discrimination is wrong and that opportunities should be more fairly distributed does not automatically translate into support for equal opportunities legislation, much less the liberal approach favoured by New Labour. We might easily suggest that in fact a large proportion, maybe even a majority, of the general population are at best indifferent to equal opportunities as a policy issue and at worst actively hostile (Levin, 1992; Saunders, 2011). Equality of opportunity is not a 'common sense' issue, it is inherently ideological (Wetherell *et al.*, 1987); as Hill (2002) has argued in relation to its connection to New Labour's education policy, it was a top-down, centralised project with neo-liberalism at its heart.

As a result, equal opportunities is conceived of as a hobby horse of the liberal elite, with no widespread support and little in the way of evidence to justify its application (Saunders, 2011). The problem that equality of opportunity is directed to eradicate is discrimination, and it is here that ideology makes its entrance into the policy-making sphere. There are those who regard discrimination as a major problem to be overcome, and they hail from very diverse points on the political spectrum, but similarly there are a lot of people who see discrimination very differently. Saunders (2011), who is one of the most vociferous critics of equal opportunities (though he would wrongly see this as formal equality and distinct from equality of opportunity), would accept that formal equal opportunities is just about tolerable, i.e. ending discrimination on the basis of characteristics such as 'race', ethnicity and gender that cannot be altered by the victim, and has no genuine place in fair decision making. Equal treatment is the best way of ensuring fairness and stopping people from engaging in irrational forms of discrimination – treating someone less favourably because of the colour of their skin or their sex. As we shall see below, this was *not* what New Labour regarded as the best way of equalising opportunities.

Still others see discrimination as simply a matter of choice and beyond the scope of governments or agencies to influence. Milton Friedman, for example, a leading light in neo-liberal economics, would see an employer who routinely denies employment to women even though they are the 'best person for the job' as harming themselves by reducing their profit margins (Friedman, 1962). Eventually, through self-interest employers and providers of goods and services will stop discriminating in order to recruit the best people and maximise their profits. However, if they elect to continue discriminating and are prepared to absorb the losses it creates, then that is their prerogative; to impose on the decision-making process of individual employers, for example to dispose of job opportunities as they see fit, is to erode fundamental freedoms. From the perspective of Levin, certainly in terms of gender, there is no point in intervening anyway because sex roles are biologically ascribed. Setting out the reasons for women taking the bulk of caring responsibilities and men carving out careers more successfully in the public sphere, he maintains that:

> It is easy to see how these differences would create economic and caretaker roles without discrimination or oppression. The new mother, more sensitive than her mate to infantile sounds, flooded with sex-specific hormones bonds with her baby. Wanting more than her mate to be with and cosset her baby she stays with it. Her superior fine-motor co-ordination and tolerance for repetition further incline her to assume these tasks. Meanwhile her mate, preferring status and control of the physical environment, is out hunting mastodons or closing a deal. Resources are used most efficiently if the mother also assumes care of whatever counts as home. (Reinforcing these choices is the undoubted preference of young children for their mothers.) It is not that, absolutely speaking, women *like* domestic tasks and *dislike* competition, and vice-versa for men; women like domestic tasks *more than men do* while men like dominance *more than women do*, and this relative difference differentiates roles. Men outrank women in the hierarchical world of work because they seek higher positions more avidly. Nor do hierarchies favour men: they favour certain traits, such as objective thinking and ruthlessness. Women who 'think like men' do achieve hierarchical success; it is just that more men than women think like men. Wanting dominance more, men work harder for it and, other things being equal, achieve it more often. And other things are not equal, because of sex differences in abilities.
>
> (Levin, 1992: 15–16, emphases in the original)

As Kohn (1992) suggests, a lot of time, effort and ink are expended trying to make us accept things that are inevitable functions of biology, that human nature is inherently competitive, for example. The implication is that if something is that engrained, it would not be necessary to sell or justify it; there would be no need. This becomes its own appeal to 'common sense', which is an attempt by all of its proponents (left, right or centre in political terms) to invalidate opposing viewpoints and perspectives. After all, who could argue against common sense? Thus many on the right of the political spectrum believe that equal opportunity policies and laws are unjust, that they are unnecessary, or that they are utterly pointless.

What this discussion underlines, both in terms of the evidence drawn from public opinions and the world views that connect them to political preferences, is that discrimination as a social problem and the acceptance of equal opportunities measures are matters of ideology, not a function of 'common sense'. Of course, to remain passive is no less ideological; the faith some have in the market is no more a function of common sense than to embrace an equal opportunities discourse or policy option. Therefore, equality of opportunity as conceived of by New Labour indicates one major weak point in their claims about basing policy only on evidence; any commitment to equality of opportunity reflects an ideological perspective.

The theory of equal opportunities: a puzzle inside an enigma

Once it is accepted that discrimination is a social problem worthy of a response, to echo our discussion above that it is ideologically important enough to require a response, the next step is to construct an *effective* response. We discussed earlier in the book the importance of knowing what a policy is designed to achieve, and this is something that has been decidedly problematic in relation to equality of opportunity. For a subject that has such a profound impact on our everyday lives, and we suspect that you would be able to name several ways in which equality of opportunity issues have influenced your life in the past week, the confusion surrounding its meaning and intentions is significant (Johns and Green, 2009). Very recently Saunders (2011) – remember a vociferous critic of equality in any form – set out the following three-point conceptual framework:

- formal equality
- equality of opportunity
- equality of outcome.

While there is some validity to this framework, a better option in our view is that provided by Forbes (1991):

- formal equality of opportunity
- liberal equality of opportunity
- radical equality of opportunity.

The different models that this framework contains have one thing in common: they are all aimed at the problem of discrimination, although the form that discrimination takes will vary according to the model in question.

We can dismiss radical equality of opportunity quite quickly, because it requires the use of positive discrimination. For those who are unclear about what positive discrimination means, for the sake of clarity it usually involves offering people from protected groups (groups that have been discriminated against) employment opportunities or educational places to compensate for that discrimination. It is positive rather than negative, although not for the unprotected individuals who now lose out. There is insufficient space to cover the complicated nature of this theoretical and policy area, but fuller accounts can be found in Bagilhole (2009) and Johns (2005, 2006). We can brush over positive discrimination because it has never been part of the legislative landscape in the UK. Of course, this has been disputed, as with so much else in the context of social science and policy making, with New Labour having written all-women shortlists for political selection for parliament into statute under the Sex Discrimination (Election Candidates) Act 2002 (Kelly and White, 2009), but this does not technically qualify as positive discrimination because it is not an offer of employment, only candidature (Lovenduski and Norris,

2003). Similarly, the provisions that require employers to guarantee an interview to qualified disabled individuals are not a guarantee of employment. Even if positive discrimination were used, it is poorly framed as 'radical' because it makes no attempt to alter society in anything but a procedural sense. Poverty and wealth would continue to exist in a world where positive discrimination were routinely used; it would simply mean a more diverse range of people would have access to the wealth (and by extension the poverty also) than is currently the case (Edwards, 1995; Johns, 2006).

Formal equality of opportunity has been the lifeblood of the legislation since the raft of measures that were passed in the 1970s, the core of which included:

- the 1970 Equal Pay Act
- the Sex Discrimination Act 1975
- the Race Relations Act 1976.

From this perspective, discrimination is the unfair treatment of one person or group of persons as against another person or group of persons, and the best way of stopping it is through limiting discretion. Cutting the room for discretion requires equal treatment and, in turn, the standardisation of procedures. When you apply for a job, you will see job descriptions, person specifications and so on, and at interview you will be asked a set range of questions in the same order and these will be scored against established criteria. The thinking is that once everyone is treated equally – that is, treated in the same way – discrimination will be eradicated.

There were, and are, serious questions about this assumption. It portrays discrimination as an individualistic phenomenon, ignoring the context and structures through which interactions occur and are interpreted. More importantly, it brushes aside the discrimination that may have impacted on a person prior to the point at which they are seeking employment, for example. Liberal equality of opportunity, one form of which is commonly known as positive action, requires differential treatment in order to get disadvantaged people to the starting line. The intention is to equalise background conditions not treatment (see Law and Harrison, 2001 for an interesting take on collective notions of positive action). Where women might be under-represented in the higher echelons of the police service, they can be offered additional training to compensate for any structural unfairness they might have experienced. Other aspects of positive action include outreach recruitment efforts and goals and targets, both of which became increasingly important in the context of criminal justice.

Positive action was always a part of the legislation, although it was peripheral and all but ignored until the arrival of New Labour (Iganski *et al.*, 2001; Law and Harrison, 2001; Johns, 2005). In many ways this was perhaps a blessing in that it meant that formal equality could operate, at least in theory, with some degree of coherence. It may have been ineffective, and judging this is not easy; would we expect to see a reduction in discrimination cases going to employment tribunals? Would it reflect higher rates of prosecution? Certainly the continued existence of discrimination has been seen as a failure of the legislation (Brown and Gay, 1985; Esmail and Everington, 1993). Whatever our own response to this question, New Labour clearly adjudged formal equality and equal treatment to be inadequate and therefore created the momentum for a major shift towards positive action in the public sector, and in doing so ironically used criminal justice as a launch pad.

Equal opportunities in practice: UK policing

The connection between policing and equal opportunities has been most sharply drawn around the issues of 'race' and racism. Until the latter part of the 1950s policing was regarded as inherently even-handed and supportive of communities, represented in the person of Dixon of Dock Green in a popular television show that ran from 1955 to 1976. Gradually this reputation was lost and complaints about racism in policing came to a head in 1981 with the Brixton riots. The result was a report by Lord Scarman (1981) which concluded that while the police service was generally fine, there were a few bad apples that spoilt the barrel. Thus racism was not regarded as institutional but was mainly a problem of low ranking police officers with correspondingly low levels of educational attainment; senior officers were too educated and cultured to harbour prejudices! The report recommended a three-point strategy:

1. Screen out the bad apples by tightening up recruitment procedures.
2. Provide cultural awareness training to serving officers in order to challenge racist attitudes.
3. Discipline officers found guilty of racism.

While the report did make some impact on policing, through the introduction of the Police and Criminal Evidence Act 1984, for example, many of the key recommendations were ignored by a Conservative government unwilling to look beyond the perceived pathology of minority ethnic communities.

Concerns about racism (and of course other forms of discrimination) in the police service continued to be expressed in academic circles and from within minority communities, but arguably only token steps were taken until the arrival of New Labour in 1997. Four years before this election victory a young black man, Stephen Lawrence, had been murdered by a gang of white youths in Eltham in south London while waiting for a bus with his friend Dwayne Brooks. Despite several leads the police failed to arrest the prime suspects, allowed vital evidence to be destroyed, and targeted Brooks as the main suspect. The Conservatives refused to countenance a public inquiry but Labour promised in opposition that they would establish one. True to their word, it was one of the first things they did in office.

Lord Macpherson of Cluny was appointed as the chair of the inquiry and it proved to be a huge undertaking. Over 100,000 pages of evidence were submitted to the inquiry, and it cost in excess of £3 million to stage (Macpherson, 1999: Appendix 1). Although it did not manage to give the suspects the trial they had evaded, the final report was regarded by many as a watershed in British 'race relations' (Parekh, 2000). Not only did it conclude that the police investigations were inadequate and that the leadership had been poor, but it also suggested that there might have been corruption involved and, most importantly for our purposes, that there was evidence of *institutional racism*:

> The collective failure of an organisation to provide an appropriate and professional service to people because of their colour, culture, or ethnic origin. It can be seen or detected in processes, attitudes and behaviour which amount to discrimination through unwitting prejudice, ignorance, thoughtlessness and racist stereotyping which disadvantage minority ethnic people.
>
> (Macpherson, 1999: 6.34)

This last claim provoked an outcry from sections of the police service, the tabloid press (McLaughlin and Murji, 1999; Neal, 2003) and 'independent' think-tanks such as Civitas (Green, 2000).

It would be possible to produce an entire book on this subject – and several have been produced (Marlow and Loveday, 2000) – but our focus is on the aftermath of the report. Just as Scarman (1981) had earlier recommended, the Macpherson Report reiterated that more training was required for serving officers, that tougher action was needed to tackle racism when found, and procedures such as stop and search should be limited and where necessary subject to greater accountability and control. It also maintained that greater diversity amongst police officers was required to challenge the distorted relationships between white police officers and service/subject communities. With more black and minority ethnic officers, misunderstandings would break down and the service would better reflect and serve a diverse British society.

The report was criticised on a number of grounds beyond the initial knee-jerk reactions. On the right, commentators such as Green (2000), supported by some Conservative MPs such as William Hague, said that it went too far and would prevent officers from doing their work effectively due to their fear of being labelled as 'racist'. On the left, there were suggestions that it had not gone far enough, and that the very nature and origins of policing were inherently racist, something that the report failed to recognise (Lea, 2000). Finally, there were concerns that the main focus of the report was wrong and that the way in which murder investigations were conducted should have received more attention (Innes, 1999).

Regardless of these criticisms, the Macpherson Report (1999) had a major impact on the policy agenda of New Labour. Almost immediately the Home Office was tasked with implementing goals and targets for black and minority recruitment into policing. Shortly after this the Race Relations (Amendment) Act 2000 was passed, ending the exemption of the police and placing greater emphasis on positive action across the public sector. Not only did New Labour commit to significant domain expansion with the inclusion of age, sexuality and religion in the existing equal opportunities framework; they drew the mishmash of 116 different provisions into what would eventually become the Equality Act 2010. The requirements on the public sector have been greatly enhanced and the push towards positive action and away from formal equality of opportunity has intensified.

Ultimately, the outcomes of these changes have perhaps not been as significant as their architects would have wanted, and although we have to take into account the reality that policies take time to unfold, as Keynes once said: 'in the long run we are all dead'. Even at the time there were doubts about the practical impact of the Macpherson Report – for example:

> The experience of the Scarman Report should warn us against making any facile predictions about the nature of the policy response that we are likely to see. If anything the experience of the last two decades teaches us that the way in which policy recommendations are translated into practice remains fundamentally uncertain, particularly as the nature of policy change depends on broader political agendas.
>
> (1999: 3.2)

The goals and targets introduced by the Home Office in 1999 were eventually abandoned. Even the unprecedented step of introducing cultural and lingual elements into recruitment procedures, as the Metropolitan Police Service did, was soon dispensed with. Nevertheless, as a result of the report, and the legislation and policy it partially inspired, there have been changes in the personnel profile of the police service as a whole (Benetto, 2009: 2):

- For all staff, both civilian and sworn officers, the police has exceeded the Home Office target for ethnic minorities to make up at least 7 per cent of the service in England and Wales by 2009. In 2007 the total was 8 per cent.
- The proportion of ethnic minority officers has risen from 2 per cent in 1999 to 3.9 per cent (5,511 officers) in April 2007. However, the target of 7 per cent will almost certainly not be met.
- The proportion of ethnic minorities who were successful police recruits increased from 6.3 per cent to 10.7 per cent of the total number of candidates during the first half of 2007–8.
- Nearly 12 per cent of police community support officers are from ethnic minority groups.
- Targets on progression through the ranks have been met, in all but the very top levels.

Despite these improvements, the question about the role of diversity in challenging racism is a difficult one. Can increased diversity, alongside training programmes, truly tackle discrimination and racism, or is it simply a means of passing responsibility for change onto victims (Johns, 2004, 2005, 2006)?

Concern was raised about ongoing problems in the police service as a whole when the BBC documentary *The Secret Policeman* was aired in 2003. This followed the experiences of a journalist who had covertly joined the police in order to explore the changes that had been implemented in police training – the results were at times shocking, with some recent recruits expressing extreme racism and promising to use their authority to actively harm BME members of the public. Disturbingly, the programme did not pick up on the institutionalised racism that was directed at an Asian colleague who was forced to drop back to an earlier stage after being fast-tracked (Rowe, 2007). Moreover, the work of Rowe (2007) has underlined the way in which proposals made by Macpherson about cultural awareness training and diversifying the workforce have been resisted in some quarters.

On the whole, after the first shock waves produced by the publication of the report and the momentum it provided for legislative and policy reform, it would be a stretch to argue that significant changes have been made to the structure and process of UK policing in the pursuit of greater equality of opportunity (Neal, 2003). At the time of writing the Metropolitan Police Service is embroiled in another round of scandal about racism; figures just released show that out of 2,270 officers accused of racist behaviour since 2007 only two have been forced to resign – meaning that their pension rights were not affected. Eight officers are on suspension, along with a civilian support worker, in connection with 10 allegations of abuse, harassment, bullying and violent conduct directed at BME individuals (Townsend, 2012). Where racism is concerned, located within a wider concern for equality of opportunity, the criminal justice system as exemplified by the police service clearly has a long way to travel. And perhaps we should not be entirely surprised by this, particularly if we consider the magnitude of the change that would be required.

Equal opportunities and the magnitude of change?

That New Labour was unable to successfully equalise opportunities in the criminal justice system, and indeed more widely, particularly in terms of socio-economic status, underlines the paradigmatic change that it would require. Hall (1993) provided a framework for evaluating the degree of change that a policy implied, and this is an invaluable means of assessing the scope of change that equality of opportunity would require in a society such as the UK. At the lowest level of change, policy is directed to alter settings, what he referred to as first-order change. Certainly equalising opportunities would require settings to alter, just as it would demand a second-order alteration of instruments. Yet, from our perspective, even the most conservative form of equality of opportunity, the formal version set out earlier, would mean far more than altering settings and instruments of policy. We suggest that equalising opportunities implies a third-order paradigmatic shift in policy.

As far back as the writings of Plato (1991), which were produced a little under 300 years before the birth of Christ, the seismic shift that would be required to equalise opportunities was recognised. In his *Republic*, where he described a society constructed around merit (a true meritocracy), the role of the family had to be altered radically as it was seen to play a significant role in preventing fair opportunities. Essentially children would have to be raised collectively in specialist institutions to ensure that their talents were recognised and that they could be streamed effectively. There were three classes with metallic values attached to them: gold as the ruling class (the Guardians), through silver as the police and military caste (the Auxiliaries) and finally the iron class, those who performed the necessary work for a society to survive. Interestingly, Plato argued that in order for this society to function effectively it needed to have an inverted material hierarchy – in effect, those at the top of society ought to be the poorest in material possessions. This would work because they would be engaged in intellectual pursuits and self-improvement and would have little interest in wealth and property.

Whether we approve of this schema or not, the point is that it was a truly radical vision that underlined the degree of change needed in Athenian society if equality of opportunity was to be achieved. Clearly it also runs counter to the way in which modern societies organise themselves, though *in principle* the end goals are the same as those of modern advocates of equal opportunities policies. New Labour set out their belief that only when opportunities are equalised can greater equality be achieved (Blond and Milbank, 2010). The stance of New Labour prompted Michael Young (2001), a famous sociologist and the person who coined the phrase 'meritocracy' which was so beloved by Blair and others in New Labour, to complain that the whole point of his book *The Rise of the Meritocracy* had been misunderstood – indeed, not misunderstood but distorted. In fact, the book was meant to be a political satire, not a blueprint for political parties to adopt. He suggested that meritocracy in a capitalist system is even more punishing for the marginalised than the feudal system it succeeded; at least a peasant could argue that his or her status was prescribed by birth, whereas under capitalism not only were the poor regarded as failures but they were also blamed for that failure. Ultimately, he argued that, rather than opportunities leading to equality, it was necessary to pursue greater equality before opportunities could be secured.

At present we are very far from implementing policies that would create anything like Plato's Republic even, and it is difficult to see such an approach materialising in the very near future. What this means is that in championing equality of opportunity New Labour were theoretically engaged in a project demanding paradigmatic change without the will to introduce policies that would produce it. Furthermore, in the criminal justice system – for the reasons we set out above – this would have been even more challenging where the constitutive institutions have limited experience (and possibly, in some quarters, little interest) in equalising opportunities. If commentators such as Lea (2000) are right, then certain components such as the police were actually constructed to control the targets of New Labour's programme, regarding them as part of the 'dangerous classes'. We would argue that it is not even necessary to accept this political perspective to see that equality of opportunity has been, and may well remain for some time, a problematic policy agenda for UK criminal justice.

Conclusion

The purpose of this chapter was to use equal opportunities as an illustrative example, drawing out some of the theories and policy-related ideas and practices explained in the earlier chapters. Taken in this way, what it shows is that, far from New Labour achieving the evidence-based approach to policy they advocated, there were areas that were strongly driven by ideological perspectives. It is hard to see how equality of opportunity could be anything other than a top-down, ideological commitment for those who subscribe to it.

Moreover, it also shows the problems policy makers have where what they seek to achieve is inadequately defined and poorly understood. As we have written elsewhere (Johns and Green, 2009), equal opportunities as law and policy, diluted by language of 'equality and diversity', is becoming ever more muddled as time progresses. This seems to indicate that while New Labour appeared to advocate a rational model, they were merely laying more layers of confusion over an already trampled field. There was more of the incremental than the rational model in the way that they proceeded, although in fairness maybe that is true of most policy programmes.

Given the degree of conceptual confusion, the slightly haphazard mode of designing and implementing equal opportunities policies, and the order of change required, it is perhaps not surprising that the achievements in inculcating equality of opportunity in the UK criminal justice system have been arguably modest. Getting agencies to acknowledge institutional discrimination is one thing, trying to get them to challenge and change it is something else entirely. Policy making, both in conception and implementation, is a complex and testing activity, and with all the obstacles in place maybe it is important to have an ideological vision, to be honest about it, and to see the journey as equally important to the eventual destination.

Questions for consideration

1. What makes equality of opportunity such an ideological concept?
2. Is the police service infected by institutional racism?
3. How would you go about equalising opportunities?
4. What order of change would be required to equalise opportunities? Is it a paradigm shift that is needed?
5. What would a society defined by equal opportunities look like?

10 Final thoughts

When completing a project, it is sometimes useful to pause and reflect on what was intended at the beginning. When discussing and planning this work, we were struck with the inability of otherwise able criminology and criminal justice students to demonstrate or articulate much in the way of meaningful knowledge about policy, but especially the processes involved in the making and implementing of policy. As a result we felt that their understanding of both the theory and the practice of their chosen subject specialism was at best partial. Practice is obvious: they need to know what, how and why criminal justice agencies do what they currently do, what, how and why they previously did what they did and, arguably most importantly for the next wave of criminologists and criminal justice practitioners, what future policy can look like, how that can be achieved and why future policy will be shaped in the manner it is. Theory and policy may not be so obvious but we believe that theory, policy and practice are linked, even if the relationship is not articulated. As Knepper (2007: 19) stresses in his attempt to connect social policy with criminological theory: 'Every theory of crime contains an argument about what should be done in response. While theories about the aetiology of crime do not always offer policy proposals as such, the theorised source of crime signals a preferred solution.'

So we set about constructing a book that went part way to filling what we see as a gap in many criminology and criminal justice courses, writing a textbook that was specifically aimed at undergraduate criminology and criminal justice students with the express intention of providing them with a basic introduction to policy, policy making and policy implementation. The book was never intended to be the definitive guide, rather it was to be used as a point of reference, a beginning point not an end point. We are aware that there are other more complete policy books but ours is unique inasmuch as it is aimed at a specific group of students so as to be relevant to their chosen field of study. Like many of these types of books, the origins lie in a module that one of us taught and that gave us an insight into the fact that policy making is best explained by using examples from real life, or creating little vignettes to reflect the lived experiences of the students, which is what we have tried to do throughout.

In the previous chapters we have covered much ground and self-confessedly we have sacrificed depth for breadth. Again, we see no need to apologise for this as the target audience is one that we assume has little or no knowledge of the intricacies or complexities of policy making but needs to know and understand policy at a basic level. In order to achieve that we have moved through theories of the state, through models of policy making, across the roles and responsibilities of government and on to the manner in which policy is implemented, measured and assessed. We are confident that on completion of this book most students will have the level of knowledge to understand at least the how and why of policy making and implementation.

All that remains is for us to make one last plea on behalf of the policy community. It is our contention that any understanding of an academic subject that has any practical application whatsoever is incomplete without a grasp of how policy makers are informed by theory, ideology, schools of thought and underpinning philosophies and then use that knowledge to craft social interventions that have direct, continuous and often far-reaching consequences on the lives of the population. The fact that very often those interventions do not fall equally or proportionally on the population makes the need to understand the processes even more pressing.

Without doubt we are living in challenging and changing times. Some of the old certainties are being swept away, new allegiances are forming and the political and policy landscape is changing, often rapidly and with anxiety-provoking consequences. It has been a long time since policy has been so interesting and so potentially transformative. Our hope is that, at worst, reading through this book and undertaking the exercises will have provided you with the skills, knowledge and analytical capabilities to appreciate the importance of this current period of flux and fully understand its implications. Of course, what we really hope for is what we see as the best case scenario: that you will use this book as a starting point to investigate the policy-making process more fully and come to appreciate the centrality of policy to all we do.

Bibliography

Abercrombie, N., Hill, S. and Turner, B.S. (1984) *The Penguin Dictionary of Sociology* (2nd edn), Harmondsworth: Penguin.

Alcock, P. (1990) 'The end of the line for social security: the Thatcherite restructuring of welfare', *Critical Social Policy*, 10(30): 88–105.

Aldridge, M. (1999) 'Probation officer training, promotional culture and the public sphere', *Public Administration*, 77(1): 77–90.

Audit Commission (1983) *Handbook on Economy, Efficiency and Effectiveness*, London: HMSO.

Bagilhole, B. (2009) *Understanding Equal Opportunities and Diversity: The Social Differentiations and Intersections of Inequality*, Bristol: The Policy Press.

Barlow, A. and Duncan, S. (2000) 'New Labour's communitarianism, supporting families and the "rationality mistake": Part II', *Journal of Social Welfare and Family Law*, 22(2): 129–43.

Barnes, M. and Prior, D. (1996) 'From private choice to public trust: a new social basis for welfare', *Public Money & Management*, 16(4): 51–7.

Barry, M. (2005) *Youth Policy and Social Inclusion*, London: Routledge.

Barton, A. (2002) *Managing Fragmentation: An Area Child Protection Committee at a Time of Change*, Aldershot: Ashgate.

——(2008) 'New Labour's management, audit and "what works" approach to controlling the "untrustworthy" professions', *Public Policy and Administration*, 23(3): 263–77.

——(2011) *Illicit Drugs: Use and Control* (2nd edn), London: Routledge.

Barton, A. and Johns, N.R. (2005) 'Pragmatism and the third way: an open door for new racism?', *Social Policy and Society*, 4(3): 283–91.

Bastable, R. and Sheather, J. (2005) 'Mandatory reporting to the police of all sexually active under-13s: new protocols may undermine confidential sexual health services for young people', *British Medical Journal*, 331(7522): 918–19.

BBC News (2006) 'Cannes director urges CCTV debate', http://news.bbc.co.uk/1/hi/entertainment/5000720.stm (accessed 30th January 2008).

——(2010) 'Prison numbers in England and Wales reach record high', http://news.bbc.co.uk/1/hi/uk/8640399.stm.

——(2011a) 'Prison numbers in England and Wales hit fresh record', http://www.bbc.co.uk/news/uk-15693164.

——(2011b) 'Rochdale child "prostitution ring" charges', 8/6/11: http://www.bbc.co.uk/news/uk-england-manchester-13694250.

Bean, P. (2010) *Legalizing Drugs*, Bristol: Policy Press.

Benetto, J. (2009) *Police and Racism: What Has Been Achieved 10 years after the Stephen Lawrence Inquiry Report?*, London: EHRC.

Beresford, P. and Croft, S. (1995) 'It's our problem too! Challenging the exclusion of poor people from poverty discourse', *Critical Social Policy*, 15(44–45): 75–95.

Beveridge,W.A. (1942) *Social Insurance and Allied Services* (Cmd 6404), London: HMSO.

Bewley-Taylor, D.R. (2003) 'Challenging the UN drug control conventions: problems and possibilities', *International Journal of Drug Policy*,14: 171–9.

Bird, S.M., Cox, D., Farewell, V.T., Goldstein, H., Holt, T. and Smith, P.C. (2005) 'Performance indicators: good, bad, and ugly', *Journal of the Royal Statistical Society Association*, 168(1): 1–27.

Blakemore, K. (1998) *Social Policy: An Introduction*, Open University Press: Buckinghamshire.

Blanchflower, D.G. and Freeman, R.B. (1994) 'Did the Thatcher reforms change British labour market performance?', in R. Barrell (ed.) *The UK Labour Market: Comparative Aspects and Institutional Developments*, Cambridge: Cambridge University Press.

Blight, G., Pulham, S. and Torpey, P. (2011) 'Arab spring: an interactive timeline of the Middle East protests', *The Guardian*, 29/11/11: http://www.guardian.co.uk/world/interactive/2011/mar/22/middle-east-protest-interactive-timeline (accessed 5/12/11).

Blond, P. and Milbank, J. (2010) 'No equality in opportunity', *The Guardian*, 27/1/10.

Botti, S. and Iyengar, S.S. (2006) 'The dark side of choice: when choice impairs social welfare', *Journal of Public Policy and Marketing*, 25(1): 24–38.

Bowling, B. and Phillips, C. (2003) 'Policing ethnic minority communities', in T. Newburn (ed.), *Handbook of Policing*, Devon: Willan Publishing.

Bradach, J.L. and Eccles, R.G. (1989) 'Price, authority, and trust: from ideal types to plural forms', *Annual Review of Sociology*, 15: 97–118.

Briggs, R. and Birdwell, J. (2009) *Radicalisation among Muslims in the UK*, MICROCON Policy Working Paper 7, Brighton: MICROCON.

Brookhuis, K.A., De Vries, G. and De Waard, D. (1991) 'The effects of mobile telephoning on driving performance', *Accident Analysis and Prevention*, 23: 309–16.

Brown, C. (1981) 'Power and democracy', in P. McNeill and C. Townley (eds) *Fundamentals of Sociology*, Cheltenham: Thornes.

Brown, C. and Gay, P. (1985) *Racial Discrimination 17 Years after the Act*, London: Policy Studies Institute.

Brownlee, I. (1998) 'New Labour – new penology? Punitive rhetoric and the limits of managerialism in criminal justice policy', *Journal of Law and Society*, 25(3): 313–35.

Budge, I., Crewe, I., McKay, D. and Newton, K. (1998) *The New British Politics*, London: Longman.

Burnham, P., Lutz, K.G., Grant, W. and Layton-Henry, Z. (2008) Research Methods in Politics (2nd edn), London: Palgrave Macmillan.

Button, M., Williamson, T. and Johnston, L. (2007) 'Too many chiefs and not enough chief executives: barriers to the development of PFI in the police service in England and Wales', *Criminology and Criminal Justice*, 7(3): 287–305.

Cameron, A., Macdonald, G., Turner, W. and Lloyd, L. (2007) 'The challenges of joint working: lessons from the Supporting People Health Pilot evaluation', *International Journal of Integrated Care*, 7: http://www.ncbi.nlm.nih.gov/pmc/articles/PMC2092398/.

Carter, N. (1989) 'Performance indicators: "backseat driving" or "hands off" control?', *Policy & Politics*, 17(2): 131–8.

Cavadino, M. and Dignan, J. (2007) *The Penal System: An Introduction* (4th edn), London: Sage.

Cawson, P., Wattam, C., Brooker, S. and Kelly, G. (2000) *Child Maltreatment in the United Kingdom: A Study of the Prevalence of Abuse and Neglect*, London: NSPCC.

Chakrabarti, S., Kennedy, H., Klug, F., McWilliams, M. and Miller, A. (2010) *Common Sense: Reflections on the Human Rights Act*, London: Liberty.

Charles, N. (2000) *Feminism, the State and Social Policy*, London: Macmillan.

Cheney, D., Skilbeck, R., Uglow, S. and Fitzpatrick, J. (eds) (2001) *Criminal Justice and the Human Rights Act 1998*, London: Jordan Ltd.

Clark, L. (2010) 'More than 7,000 parents hit by truancy convictions as courts punish soaring levels of school absenteeism', *Mail Online*, 25/4/10: http://www.dailymail.co.uk/news/article-1268792/More-7-000-parents-hit-truancy-convictions-courts-punish-soaring-levels-school-absenteeism.html.

Clark, T. and Salaman, G. (1998) 'Telling tales: management gurus' narratives and the construction of managerial identity', *Journal of Management Studies*, 35(2): 137–61.

Clarke, J. (2004) 'Producing transparency? Evaluation and the governance of public services', in G. Drewry, C. Greve and T. Tanquerel (eds) *Contracts, Performance and Accountability*, Amsterdam: IOS Press.

Clarke, J., Gewirtz, S., Hughes, G. and Humphrey, J. (2000) 'Guarding the public interest? Auditing public services', in J. Clarke, S. Gewirtz and E. McLaughlin (eds) *New Managerialism, New Welfare?* London: Sage.

Clarke, J. and Newman, M. (1997) *The Managerial State*, London: Sage.

Coates, D. (ed.) (2003) *Paving the Third Way: The Critique of Parliamentary Socialism*, London: Merlin Press.

Cohen, P. (2003) 'The drug prohibition church and the adventure of reformation', *International Journal of Drug Policy*, 14(2): 213–15.

Cohen, S. (2002a) 'Dining with the devil: the 1999 Immigration and Asylum Act and the voluntary sector', in S. Cohen, B. Humphries and E. Mynott (eds) *From Immigration Controls to Welfare Controls*, London: Routledge.

——(2002b) 'The local state of immigration controls', *Critical Social Policy*, 22(3): 518–43.

Colebatch, H.K. (1998) *Policy*, London: Sage.

——(2002) *Policy* (2nd edn), Maidenhead: Open University Press.

Crawford, A. (1995) 'Appeals to community and crime prevention', *Crime, Law, and Social Change*, 22: 97–126.

Crawford, A. and Newburn, T. (2002) 'Recent developments in restorative justice for young people in England and Wales: community participation and representation', *British Journal of Criminology*, 43(2): 476–93.

Critcher, C. (2003) *Moral Panics and the Media*, Oxford: Oxford University Press.

Cunningham, G. (1963) 'Policy and practice', *Public Administration*, 41: 229–38.

Cutler, T. and Waine, B. (2000) 'Managerialism reformed? New Labour and public sector management', *Social Policy and Administration*, 34(3): 318–32.

Dahl, R.A. (1961) *Who Governs?*, New Haven, CT: Yale University Press.

David, M. (1983) *Parents, Gender and Education Reform*, Cambridge: Polity.

——(1985) 'Motherhood and social policy: a matter of education?', *Critical Social Policy*, 12: 28–44.

Davies, M., Croall, H. and Tyrer, J. (1998) *Criminal Justice: An Introduction to the Criminal Justice System in England and Wales* (2nd edn), London: Longman.

Dean, H. (2004) 'Popular discourse and the ethical deficiency of "third way" conceptions of citizenship', *Citizenship Studies*, 8(1): 65–82.

Dell, E. (2000) *A Strange Eventful History: Democratic Socialism in Britain*, London: HarperCollins.

Devon and Cornwall Police (2006) www.devon-cornwall.police.uk/v3/publrep/Annual
PolicingStratPlan/13performance.html (accessed 18.9.06).

Donsbach, W., Jandura, O. and Muller, D. (2005) 'War reporters or willing propagandists? How German and American print media saw "embedded journalists" in the Iraq War', *Medien & Kommunikationswissenschaft*, 53(2–3): 298.

Dorey, P. (2005) *Policy Making in Britain: An Introduction*, London: Sage.

Dorling, D. (2010) *Injustice: Why Social Inequality Persists*, Bristol: The Policy Press.

Douglas, A. (2008) *Partnership Working*, London: Routledge.

Duke, K. (2001) 'Evidence-based policy making? The interplay between research and the development of prison drugs policy', *Criminology and Criminal Justice*, 1(3): 277–300.

Dworkin, R.M. (ed.) (1977) *The Philosophy of Law: Oxford Readings in Philosophy*, Oxford: Oxford University Press.

Eagleton, T. (2007) *Ideology: An Introduction*, London: Verso.

Eaton, G. (2011) 'Police cuts: even worse than expected', *New Statesman The Staggers*, 21/7/11: http://www.newstatesman.com/blogs/the-staggers/2011/07/front-line-cuts-police.

Edelman, M. (2001) *The Politics of Misinformation*, Cambridge: Cambridge University Press.

Edwards, J. (1995) *When Race Counts*, London: Routledge.

Enthoven, A.C. (1991) 'Internal market reform of the British National Health Service', *Health Affairs*, 10(3): 60–70.

Esmail, A., Everington, S. (1993) 'Racial discrimination against doctors from ethnic minorities', *British Medical Journal*, 306: 691–2.

Fairclough, N. (2000) *New Labour, New Language?* London: Routledge.

Falkner, G. (1998) *EU Social Policy in the 1990s: Towards a Corporatist Policy Community*, London: Routledge.

Faulkner, D. (2011) 'Criminal justice reform at a time of austerity: what needs to be done?', in A. Silvestri (ed.) *Lessons for the Coalition: An End of Term Report on New Labour and Criminal Justice*, London: Centre for Crime and Justice Studies.

Finch, N. (2004) 'Family Policy in the UK', third report for the project Welfare Policy and Employment in the Context of Family Change, University of York, www-users.york.ac.uk/~jrb1./.

Flint, C. (2006) *Introduction to Geopolitics*, London: Routledge.

Flynn, N. (1997) *Public Sector Management*, Hemel Hempstead: Harvester Wheatsheaf.

Foley, M. (2000) *The British Presidency* (2nd edn), Manchester: Manchester University Press.

Forbes, I. (1991) 'Equal opportunity: radical, liberal and conservative critiques', in E. Meehan and S. Sevenhuijsen (eds) *Equality, Politics and Gender*, London: Sage.

Forbes, S. and Ames, E. (2012) *The Freedom Manifesto: Why Markets Are Moral and Big Government Isn't*, New York: Crown Business.

Foster, P. and Wilding, P. (2000) 'Whither Welfare Professionalism?', *Social Policy and Administration*, 34(2): 143–59.

Freeden, M. (1999) 'The ideology of New Labour', *Political Quarterly*, 70(1): 42–51.

Friedman, M. (1962) *Capitalism and Freedom*, Chicago, IL: University of Chicago Press.

Galston, W.A. (2002) 'Accommodating community: expressive freedom of association in a liberal pluralist state', *The Responsive Community*, 12(3): 13–26.

——(2005) *The Practice of Liberal Pluralism*, Cambridge: Cambridge University Press.

Gamble, A. (1988) 'Privatization, Thatcherism and the British state', *Journal of Law and Society*, 16(1): 1–20.

Garboden, M. (2010) 'Baby Peter case in Haringey', *Community Care*, 9/12/10: http://www.communitycare.co.uk/Articles/09/12/2010/109961/baby-peter-case-in-haringey.htm.

Garland, D. and Sparks, R. (2000) 'Criminology, social theory and the challenge of our times', *British Journal of Criminology*, 40(2): 189–204.

Garthwaite, K. (2011) 'The language of shirkers and scroungers? Talking about illness, disability and coalition welfare reform', *Disability & Society*, 26(3): 369–72.

George, V. and Wilding, P. (1994) *Welfare and Ideology*, London: Harvester Wheatsheaf.

Gewirtz, S. (2001) 'Cloning the Blairs: New Labour's programme for the re-socialization of working-class parents', *Journal of Education Policy*, 16(4): 365–78.

Gibbs, J.P. (1968) 'Definitions of law and empirical questions', *Law and Society Review*, 2(3): 429–46.

Giddens, A. (1998) *The Third Way: The Renewal of Social Democracy*, Cambridge: Polity.

——(2000) *The Third Way and Its Critics*, Cambridge, UK: Polity.

Gilbert, R., Kemp, A., Thoburn, J., Sidebotham, P., Radford, L., Glaser, D. and MacMillan, H. (2009) 'Recognising and responding to child maltreatment', *The Lancet*, 373: 167–80.

Gillies, V. (2005) 'Meeting parents' needs? Discourses of "support" and "inclusion" in family policy', *Critical Social Policy*, 25(1): 70–90.

Gilmour, I. (1992) *Dancing with Dogma: Britain under Thatcherism*, London: Pocket Books.

Glatter, R. (2003) 'Collaboration, collaboration, collaboration', *Management in Education*, 17(5): 16–20.

Glennerster, H. (2006) *British Social Policy: 1945 to the Present* (3rd edn), Oxford: Wiley-Blackwell.

Gordon, J. (ed.) (2001) *Solar Energy: The State of the Art*, Oxford: Earthscan.

Gramsci, A. (1971) *Selections from the Prison Notebooks*, London: Lawrence & Wishart.

Green, G.D. (ed.) (2000) *Institutional Racism and the Police: Fact or Fiction?*, London: Institute for the Study of Civil Society.

Grimshaw, R. (2004) 'Whose justice? Principal drivers of criminal justice policy, their implications for stakeholders, and some foundations for critical policy departures', *British Society of Criminology Journal*, 7: http://www.britsoccrim.org/volume7/005.pdf (accessed 1/10/06).

Habermas, J. (1976) *Legitimation Crisis*, London: Heinemann.

Haigney, D.E., Taylor, R.G. and Westerman, S.J. (2000) 'Concurrent mobile (cellular) phone use and driving performance: task demand characteristics and compensatory processes', *Transport Research Part F*, 3: 113–21.

Hall, P. (1993) 'Policy paradigms, social learning and the state: the case of economic policymaking in Britain', *Comparative Politics*, 25(3): 275–96.

Hall, S. (2003) 'New Labour's double-shuffle', *Soundings*, 24: 10–24.

Ham, C. (1982) *Health Policy in Britain: The Politics and Organisation of the National Health Service*, London: Macmillan.

Harrison, B. (1999) 'The rise, fall and rise of political consensus in Britain since 1940', *History*, 84(274): 301–24.

Hayek, F.A. (1944) *The Road to Serfdom*, London: George Routledge and Sons.

Heffernan, R. (2001) *New Labour and Thatcherism: Political Change in Britain*, London: Palgrave Macmillan.

——(2003) 'Prime ministerial predominance? Core executive politics in the UK', *British Journal of Politics and International Relations*, 5(3): 347–72.

Heilbroner, R. (1998) *The Worldly Philosophers: The Lives, Times and Ideas of the Great Economic Thinkers*, New York: Simon and Schuster.

Helfer, R.E. and Kempe, C.H. (eds) (1976) *Child Abuse and Neglect: The Family and the Community*, Cambridge, MA: Ballinger.

Henry III, W.A. (1994) *In Defense of Elitism*, New York: Anchor Books/Doubleday.

Hill, D. (2002) '"Education, education, education", or "business, business, business"? The third way ideology of New Labour's educational policy in England and Wales', Paper presented at the European Conference on Educational Research, Lahti, Finland, 22–25 September 1999: http://www.leeds.ac.uk/educol/documents/00002208.htm (accessed 12/4/01).

Hill, M. (1997) *The Policy Process in the Modern State*, London: Prentice-Hall.

——(2005) *The Public Policy Process* (4th edn), Harlow: Pearson Education, Harlow Government Office (2006), www.directgov.uk.

Hillyard, P. (1993) *Suspect Community: People's Experience of the Prevention of Terrorism Acts in Britain*, London: Pluto Press with Liberty.

——(2005) 'The "War on Terror": Lessons from Ireland', http://www.ecln.org/essays/essays-1.pdf.

Holdaway, S. and O'Neill, M. (2006) 'Institutional racism after Macpherson: an analysis of police views', *Policing and Society*, 16(4): 349–69.

Home Office (2004) 'Updated Drug Strategy', www.drugs.gov.uk/drugstrategy/ (accessed 09.05.06).

——(2010) *Integrated Offender Management: Key Principles*, London: Stationery Office.

Hood, C. (1995) 'The "New Public Management" in the eighties', *Accounting, Organization and Society*, 20(2/3): 93–109.

Hope, C. and Hughes, M. (2012) 'David Cameron hosted dinners for millionaire donors in Downing Street flat', *Daily Telegraph*, 26/3/12.

House of Commons Constitutional Affairs Committee (2007) *The Creation of the Ministry of Justice: Sixth Report of Session 2006–07*, London: The Stationery Office Ltd.

Hudson, B. (1987) 'Collaboration in social welfare: a framework for analysis', *Police and Politics*, 15(3): 175–82.

Humphries, B. (2004) 'An unacceptable role for social work: implementing immigration policy', *British Journal of Social Work*, 34: 93–107.

Hunte, J. (1965) *Nigger Hunting in England?* London: West Indian Standing Conference.

Hunter, D. (2009) 'The case against choice and competition', *Health Economics, Policy and Law*, 4(4): 48–501.

Iganski, P., Mason, D., Humphreys, A. and Watkins, M. (2001) 'Equal opportunities and positive action in the British National Health Service: some lessons from the recruitment of minority ethnic groups to nursing and midwifery', *Ethnic and Racial Studies*, 42(2): 294–317.

Innes, M. (1999) 'Beyond the Macpherson report: managing murder inquiries in context', *Sociological Research Online*, 4(1): http://www.socresonline.org.uk/4/lawrence/innes.html.

Ismaili, K. (2006) 'Contextualizing the criminal justice policy-making process', *Criminal Justice Policy Review*, 17(3): 255–69.

James, A. and Raine, J. (1998) *The New Politics of Criminal Justice*, London: Longman.

Jewson, N., Mason, D., Lambkin, C. and Taylor, F. (1992) *Ethnic Monitoring Policy and Practice: A Study of Employers' Experiences*, Research Paper No. 89, London: Department of Employment.

Jha, A. (2011) 'Age of criminal responsibility is too low, say brain scientists', *The Guardian*, 13/12/11.

Johns, N.R. (1999) 'Lawrence Report: an old present newly wrapped', *Crime Prevention and Community Safety: An International Journal*, 1(2): 47–50.
——(2004) 'Ethnic diversity policy: perceptions within the NHS', *Social Policy and Administration*, 38(1): 73–88.
——(2005) 'Positive action and the problem of merit: employment policies in the National Health Service', *Critical Social Policy*, 25(2): 139–63.
——(2006) *How the British National Health Service Deals with Ethnic Diversity: Professional Problems, Patient Problems*, New York: Edwin Mellen.
Johns, N.R. and Green, A. (2009) 'Equal opportunity: obfuscation as social justice', *Equal Opportunities International*, 28(4): 289–303.
Johns, N.R., Hyde, M. and Barton, A. (2010) 'Diversity or solidarity? Making sense of the "new" social democracy', *Diversity* (open access): http://mdpi.com/journal/diversity/special_issues/ethnic-diversity.
Johns, N.R., Green, A.J., Barton, A. and Squire, G. (2012) *Trust and Substitutes for Trust: The Case of Britain under New Labour*, New York: Nova Science.
Jolley, R. (2007) '85% of public say "narrow the gap Gordon"', http://www.fabians.org.uk/publications/extracts/rachael-jolley (accessed 13/2/12).
Jones, T. and Garland, D. (2005) 'Comparative criminal justice policy-making in the United States and the United Kingdom: the case of private prisons', *British Journal of Criminology*, 45(1): 58–80.
Jones, T. and Newburn, T. (2002) 'The transformation of policing? Understanding current trends in policing systems', *British Journal of Criminology*, 42: 129–46.
Jordan, B. (2001) 'Tough love: social work, social exclusion and the third way', *British Journal of Social Work*, 31: 527–46.
Kantola, J. and Squires, J. (2004) 'Discourses surrounding prostitution policies in the UK', *European Journal of Women's Studies*, 11(1): 77–101.
Kavanagh, D., Richards, D., Smith, M. and Geddes, A. (2005) *British Politics* (5th edn), Oxford: Oxford University Press.
Kelly, R. and White, I. (2009) 'All-women shortlists', SN/PC/05057: www.parliament.uk/briefing-papers/SN05057.pdf (accessed 23/2/11).
King, D. (1987) *The New Right: Politics, Markets, and Citizenship*, London: Macmillan.
Kingdon, J.W. (1984) *Agendas, Alternatives and Public Policies*, New York: HarperCollins.
Klein, R. (1989) *The Politics of the National Health Service* (2nd edn), London: Longman.
Knepper, P. (2007) *Criminology and Social Policy*, London: Sage.
Kohn, A. (1992) *No Contest: The Case against Competition* (2nd edn), Boston, MA: Houghton Mifflin.
Landman, T. (2008) 'Imminence and proportionality: The U.S. and U.K. responses to global terrorism', *California Western International Law Journal*, 38: 75–106.
Law, I. and Harrison, M. (2001) 'Positive action, particularism and practice', *Policy Studies*, 22(1): 35–50.
Lea, John (2000) 'The Macpherson report and the question of institutional racism', *Howard Journal of Criminal Justice*, 39(3): 219–33.
Leavitt, G. (1999) 'Criminological theory as an art form: implications for criminal justice policy', *Crime & Delinquency*, 45(3): 389–99.
Le Grand, J. (1991) *Equity and Choice: An Essay in Economics and Applied Philosophy*, London: Routledge.
——(1997) 'Knights, knaves or pawns? Human behaviour and social policy', *Journal of Social Policy*, 26(2): 149–69.
——(1998) 'The third way begins with Cora', *New Statesman*, 6 (March): 26–7.

——(2007) *The Other Invisible Hand: Delivering Public Services through Choice and Competition*, Princeton, NJ: Princeton University Press.

Levin, M. (1992) 'Women, work, biology and justice', in C. Quest (ed.) *Equal Opportunities: A Feminist Fallacy (Choice in Welfare)*, London: IEA.

Levitas, R. (1986) *The Ideology of the New Right*, Cambridge: Polity Press.

——(2004) 'Let's hear it for Humpty: social exclusion, the third way and cultural capital', *Cultural Trends*, 13(2): 41–56.

Lewis, J. (1998) 'The problem of lone-parent families in twentieth century Britain', *Journal of Social Welfare and Family Law*, 20(3): 251–83.

Lind, M. (1994) 'In defense of liberal nationalism', *Foreign Affairs*, 23: 87–99.

Lindblom, C.E. (1959) 'The science of "muddling through"', *Public Administration Review*, 19(2): 79–88.

Ling, T. (1998) *The British State since 1945: An Introduction*, Cambridge: Polity.

——(2002) 'Delivering joined-up government in the UK: dimensions, issues and problems', *Public Administration*, 80(4): 615–42.

Lipsky, M. (1980) *Street Level Bureaucracy*, New York: Russell Sage.

——(2010) *Street-Level Bureaucracy: Dilemmas of the Individual in Public Service* (2nd edn), New York: Russell Sage Foundation.

Lister, R. (1998) 'From equality to social inclusion', *Critical Social Policy*, 18(2): 215–25.

——(2001) 'New Labour: a study in ambiguity from a position of ambivalence', *Critical Social Policy*, 21(4): 425–47.

Lloyd, G., Stead, J. and Kendrick, A. (2001) *Hanging on in There: A Study of Inter-agency Work to Prevent School Exclusion in Three Local Authorities*, London: NCB.

Long, M. (2003) 'Leadership and performance management', in T. Newburn (ed.) *Handbook of Policing*, Cullompton: Willan Publishing.

Lorbiecki, A. and Jack, G. (2000) 'Critical turns in the evolution of diversity management', *British Journal of Management*, 11: S17–S31.

Loveday, B. (2000) 'Policing performance', *Criminal Justice Matters*, 40: 23–4.

Lovenduski, J. and Norris, P. (2003) 'Westminster women: the politics of presence', *Political Studies*, 51: 84–102.

Lowe, R. (1995) 'The rediscovery of poverty and the creation of the child poverty action group, 1962–68', *Contemporary Record*, 9(3): 602–11.

Lukes, S. (2004) *Power: A Radical View* (2nd edn), London: Palgrave Macmillan.

McGowan, P. (2008) 'Chief Constable backs pounding the beat and collaring villains', *Cumberland News*, 19/8/08.

McInnes, K. (2007) *A Practitioner's Guide to Interagency Working in Children's Centres: A Review of Literature*, London: Barnardo's.

McLaughlin, E. (1993) 'Controlling the bill: restructuring the police in the 1990s', *Critical Social Policy*, 13(37): 95–103.

McLaughlin, E. and Muncie, J. (2000) 'The criminal justice system: New Labour's new partnerships', in J. Clarke, S. Gewirtz and E. McLaughlin (eds) *New Managerialism, New Welfare?* London: Sage.

McLaughlin, E. and Murji, K. (1999) 'After the Stephen Lawrence Report', *Critical Social Policy*, 19(3): 371–85.

Macpherson, C.B. (1980) 'Pluralism, individualism, and participation', *Economic and Industrial Democracy*, 1(1): 21–30.

Macpherson, W., Sir (1999) *The Stephen Lawrence Enquiry*, Cm 4262, London: HMSO.

McSmith, A. (2009) 'Career politicians take over Commons', *The Independent*, 31/8/09.

Marchak, P. (1991) *The Integrated Circus: The New Right and the Restructuring of Global Markets*, Montreal: McGill Queen's University Press.

Marlow, A. and Loveday, B. (eds) (2000) *After Macpherson: Policing after the Stephen Lawrence Inquiry*, Lyme Regis: Russell House Publishing.

Marshall, T.H. (1950) *Citizenship and Social Class and Other Essays*, Cambridge: Cambridge University Press.

Mawby, R.C. and Worthington, S. (2002) 'Marketing the police – from a force to a service', *Journal of Marketing Management*, 18(9/10): 857–77.

Meer, N., Dwyer, C. and Modood, T. (2010) 'Beyond "angry Muslims"? Reporting Muslim voices in the British press', *Journal of Media and Religion*, 9: 216–31.

Metcalf, H., Anderson, T. and Rolfe, H. (2001) *Part One: Barriers to Employment for Offenders and Ex-offenders*, Research Report No. 155, London: HMSO on behalf of the Department for Work and Pensions.

Middlemas, K. (1979) *Politics in an Industrial Society*, London: Deutsch.

Milliband, R. (1972) *Parliamentary Socialism*, London: Merlin.

Millie, A. (2008) 'Crime as an issue during the 2005 UK general election', *Crime Media Culture*, 4(1): 101–112.

Ministry of Justice (2007) http://www.justice.gov.uk/about/ministers.htm.

Mitrany, D. (1934) 'The political consequences of economic planning', *The Sociological Review*, 26(4): 321–45.

Monaghan, M. (2008) 'Appreciating cannabis: the paradox of "evidence" in evidence-based policymaking', *Evidence and Policy*, 4(2): 209–31.

Morley, D. and Chen, K.H. (eds) (1996) *Stuart Hall: Critical Dialogues in Cultural Studies*, London: Routledge.

Mulholland, H. and Tempest, M. (2006) 'System "not fit for purpose," says Reid', *The Guardian*, 23/5/06.

Muncie, J. (2006) 'Governing young people: coherence and contradiction in contemporary youth justice', *Critical Social Policy*, 26(4): 770–93.

Murray, C. (1990a) 'The British underclass', *Public Interest*, 99: 4–28.

——(1990b) *The Emerging Underclass*, London: Institute of Economic Affairs.

——(1999) *The Underclass Revisited*, Washington, DC: AIE Press.

——(2001a) 'The British underclass: ten years later', *Public Interest*, 145: 25–37.

——(2001b) *Underclass + 10*, London: Civitas.

Neal, Sarah (2003) 'The Scarman Report, the Macpherson Report and the media: how newspapers respond to race-centred social policy interventions', *Journal of Social Policy*, 32(1): 55–74.

Newburn, T. and Reiner, R. (2007) 'Crime and penal policy' in A. Seldon (ed.) *Blair's Britain, 1997–2007*, Cambridge: Cambridge University Press.

Newman, J. (2001) *Modernising Governance: New Labour, Policy and Society*, London: Sage.

O'Connor, J. (2002) *The Fiscal Crisis of the State*, London: Transaction.

Office of the First Minister and Deputy First Minister (2003) *A Practical Guide to Policy Making in Northern Ireland*, Belfast: OFMDF.

OFSTED/Healthcare Commission/HMIC (2009) *Review of Services for Children and Young People, with Particular Reference to Safeguarding*, Joint Area Review, Haringey Children's Services Authority Area. London: OFSTED/Healthcare Commission/HMIC.

Organization for Economic Co-operation and Development (OECD) (2011) *Economic Policy Reforms 2010: Going for Growth*, Paris: OECD.

Orwell, G. (2004) *Nineteen Eighty-Four*, London: Penguin.

Osborne, S.P. (1997) 'Managing the coordination of social services in the mixed economy of welfare: competition, cooperation or common cause?', *British Journal of Management*, 8(4): 317–28.

Parekh, B. (2000) *The Future of Multi-ethnic Britain: The Parekh Report*, London: Profile Books.

Parsons, W. (1995) *Public Policy: An Introduction to the Theory and Practice of Policy Analysis*, Cheltenham: Edward Elgar.

——(2002) 'From muddling through to muddling up: evidence based policy-making and the modernisation of British government', *Public Policy and Administration*, 17(3): 43–60.

Paterson, C. (2007) 'Street-level surveillance: human agency and the electronic monitoring of offenders', *Surveillance and Society*, 4(2–3): 314–28.

Pattinson, S. (1997) *The Faith of the Managers: When Management Becomes Religion*, London: Cassell.

Paul, K. (1997) *Whitewashing Britain: Race and Citizenship in the Postwar Era*, New York: Cornell University Press.

Pemberton, H. (2000) 'Policy networks and policy learning: UK economic policy in the 1960s and 1970s', *Public Administration*, 78(4): 771–92.

Perrone, D. and Pratt, T.C. (2003) 'Comparing the quality of confinement and cost-effectiveness of public versus private prisons: what we know, why we do not know more, and where to go from here', *The Prison Journal*, 83: 301–22.

Peters, G. and Pierre, J. (2000) 'Citizens versus the New Public Manager: the problem of mutual empowerment', *Administration & Society*, 32(1): 9–28.

Phoenix, J. (ed.) (2009) *Regulating Sex for Sale: Prostitution Policy Reform in the UK*, Bristol: The Policy Press.

Pilger, J. (2002) *The New Rulers of the World*, London: Verso.

Pimlott, B. (1988) 'The myth of consensus', in L. Smith (ed.) *The Making of Britain: Echoes of Greatness*, Basingstoke: Macmillan.

Plant, R. (1985) 'Welfare and the value of liberty', *Government and Opposition*, 20(3): 297–314.

Plato (1991) *The Republic*, London: Vintage.

Platt, T. (1984) 'Criminology in the 1980s: progressive alternatives to "law and order"', *Crime and Social Justice*, 21–22: 191–9.

Pollitt, C. (2003) 'Joined-up government: a survey', *Political Studies Review*, 1(1): 34–49.

Powell, M. (2000) 'New Labour and the third way in the British welfare state: a new and distinctive approach?', *Critical Social Policy*, 20(1): 39–60.

Power, M. (1997) *The Audit Society: Rituals of Verification*, Oxford: Clarendon Press.

RAC (2011) *RAC Report on Motoring 2011*, London: RAC.

Reddaway, W.B. (2007) 'Problems and prospects for the UK economy', *Economic Record*, 59(3): 220–31.

Reiner, R. (1995) 'From sacred to profane: the thirty years' war of the British police', *Policing and Society: An International Journal of Research and Policy*, 5(2): 121–8.

——(2000) *The Politics of the Police* (3rd edn), Oxford: Oxford University Press.

Rhodes, R.A.W. (1994) 'The hollowing out of the state: the changing nature of the public service in Britain', *Political Quarterly*, 65(2): 138–51.

Richardson, J. (1996) 'Policy-making in the EU', in J. Richardson (ed.) *European Union: Power and Policy-making*, London: Routledge.

Rowe, M. (2004) *Policing: Race and Racism*, Cullompton: Willan Publishing.

——(ed.) (2007) *Policing beyond Macpherson*, Cullompton: Willan Publishing.

Royal College of Psychiatrists (2010) 'Child abuse and neglect: the emotional effects', Factsheet for Parents and Teachers, No. 19, http://www.rcpsych.ac.uk/pdf/Sheet19.pdf.

Sandbrook, D. (2011) 'Why today's politicians are too posh (and I don't just mean the Tories)', *Daily Mail*, 27/1/11.

Saunders, P. (1989) *Social Class and Stratification*, London: Routledge.

——(2010) *Social Mobility Myths*, London: Civitas.

——(2011) *The Rise of the Equalities Industry*, London: Civitas.

Scarman, L. (1981) *The Scarman Report*, London: HMSO.

Schlesinger, P. (1981) '"Terrorism", the media and the liberal democratic state: a critique of the orthodoxy', *Social Research*, 48(1): 74.

Schneider, S.H. (1997) 'Integrated assessment modelling of global climate change: transparent rational tool for policy making or opaque screen hiding value-laden assumptions', *Environmental Modelling Assessment*, 2: 229–49.

Scott, J. (1991) *Who Rules Britain?*, Cambridge: Polity.

——(1996) *Stratification and Power*, Bristol: Policy Press.

Seldon, A. (2010) *Trust: How We Lost It and How We Can Get It Back* (2nd edn), London: Biteback.

Self, P. (1993) *Government by the Market? The Politics of Public Choice*, London: Palgrave Macmillan.

Senior, P., Wong, K., Culshaw, A., Ellingworth, D., O'Keeffe, C. and Meadows, L. (2011) *Process Evaluation of Five Integrated Offender Management Pioneer Areas*, London: Home Office/Ministry of Justice.

Short, C. (2004) 'Clare Short: at the court of King Tony', *The Independent*, 25/10/04.

Slack, J. (2012) 'Why using private firms could help the police get more bobbies on the beat', *Mailonline*, 5/3/12: http://www.dailymail.co.uk/debate/article-2110423/West-Midlands-Surrey-Police-privatisation-help-bobbies-beat.html.

Smith, D.J. and Gray, J. (1985) *Police and People in London*, London: Gower.

Smith, M.J. (2010) 'From big government to big society: changing the state–society balance', *Parliamentary Affairs*, 63(4): 818–33.

Solesbury, W. (2001) 'Evidence based policy: whence it came and where it's going', Working Paper, London: ESRC Centre for Evidence Based Policy and Practice.

Solomon, E. (2004) *A Measure of Success: An Analysis of the Prison Service's Performance against Its Key Performance Indicators 2003–2004*, London: Prison Reform Trust.

Solomos, J. (1999) 'Social research and the Stephen Lawrence inquiry', *Sociological Research Online*, 4(1).

Sorrell, T. (1997) 'Morality, consumerism and the internal market in health care', *Journal of Medical Ethics*, 23: 71–6.

Sparrow, A. (2011) 'Politicians condemn Tottenham riots', *The Guardian*, 7/8/11.

Stella, P. (2001) 'The purpose and effects of punishment', *European Journal of Crime, Criminal Law and Criminal Justice*, 9(1): 56–68.

Stoker, G. (1998) 'Governance as theory: five propositions', *International Social Science Journal*, 50(155): 17–28.

Sullivan, R.R. (1998) 'The politics of British policing in the Thatcher/Major state', *Howard Journal of Criminal Justice*, 37(3): 306–18.

Thomas, P.A. (2002) '9/11: USA and UK', *Fordham International Law Journal*, 26(4): 1193–1233.

Timmins, N. (2001) *The Five Giants* (2nd edn), London: HarperCollins.

Townsend, M. (2012) 'Senior officer calls for watchdog after Met police racism revelations', *The Guardian*, 7/4/12.

Travis, A. (2011) '£5m scheme to divert mentally ill offenders from prison', *The Guardian*, 28/11/11.

Travis, A. and Jowit, J. (2012) 'Police privatisation plans defended by senior officers', *The Guardian*, 4/3/12.

Treffner, P.J. and Barrett, R. (2004) 'Hands-free mobile phone speech while driving degrades coordination and control', *Transportation Research Part F*, 7: 229–46.

Vertigans, S. (2010) 'British Muslims and the UK government's "war on terror" within: evidence of a clash of civilizations or emergent de-civilizing processes', *British Journal of Sociology*, 61(1): 26–44.

Victor, J.S. (1998) 'Moral panics and the social construction of deviant behaviour: a theory and application to the case of ritual child abuse', *Sociological Perspectives*, 41(3): 541–65.

Waddington, P.A.J. (1999) '"Discretion," "respectability" and institutional police racism', *Sociological Research Online*, 4(1).

Walker, S., Spohn, C. and Delone, M. (2003) *The Color of Justice: Race, Ethnicity and Crime in America* (3rd edn), London: Wadsworth.

Walmsley, K. (2007) *World Prison Population List* (6th edn), London: King's College London International Centre for Prison Studies.

Warmington, P., Daniels, H., Edwards, A., Leadbetter, J., Martin, D., Brown, S. and Middleton, D. (2004) 'Learning in and for interagency working: conceptual tensions in "joined up" practice', Paper presented to the Teaching and Learning Research Programme (TLRP) annual conference, Cardiff, November 2004.

Webb, R. and Vulliamy, G. (2001) 'The primary teacher's role in child protection', *British Educational Research Journal*, 27(1): 59–77.

Webster, W. (2009) 'CCTV policy in the UK: reconsidering the evidence base', *Surveillance and Society*, 6(1): 10–22.

Weir, S. and Beetham, D. (1999) *Political Power and Democratic Control in Britain*, London: Routledge.

Wells, P. (2004) 'New Labour and evidence based policy making', Paper presented to the PERC research seminar, 16 May 2004.

Wetherell, M., Siven, H. and Potter, J. (1987) 'Unequal egalitarianism: a preliminary study of discourses concerning gender and employment opportunities', *British Journal of Social Psychology*, 26: 59–71.

White, J. (2012) 'Olympians' pride that reveals our prejudice', *Daily Telegraph*, 12/4/12.

Wilkinson, R. and Pickett, K. (2009) *The Spirit Level: Why More Equal Societies Always Do Better*, London: Allen Lane.

Williams-Thomas, M. (2010) 'I posed as a girl of 14 online: what followed will sicken you', *Mail Online*, 11/3/10: http://www.dailymail.co.uk/news/article-1256793/I-posed-girl-14-online-What-followed-sicken-you.html.

Wolfe, J. (1991) 'State power and ideology in Britain: Mrs Thatcher's privatization programme', *Political Studies*, 39(2): 237–52.

Young, M. (1961) *The Rise of the Meritocracy, 1870–2033: An Essay on Education and Equality*, London: Penguin.

——(2001) 'Down with meritocracy', *The Guardian*, 29/6/01.

Index

Page numbers in **bold** refer to figures, page numbers in *italic* refer to tables